P9-DEL-992

Praise for *Your Survival Instinct Is Killing You*

"Not only is *Your Survival Instinct Is Killing You* endlessly fascinating and readable, but it has applicability to every human being, young or old. This book actually fills you with hope while giving you the tools you need to create the changes you want—and is filled with insights and useful examples about what makes us tick."

—Betsy Brown Braun, child development and behavior specialist, author of the bestselling book *Just Tell Me What to Say* and *You're Not the Boss of Me*

"Most of us make the mistake of thinking that life is all about happiness—not realizing that so much of what we see, feel, and do is colored not by the desire to be happy, but by the very real and hard-wired need to be *safe*. Until we understand this basic fact about ourselves—and, thanks to Dr. Schoen, what we can do about it—we can't begin to truly thrive."

—Heidi Grant Halvorson, Ph.D., author of *Succeed* and coauthor of *Focus*

"This is an incredibly informative, exciting, and useful book for lay readers concerned about their own health as well as health-care professionals treating patients wishing to learn a new approach. Dr. Schoen explains how we can develop a new relationship with 'discomfort,' which is at the heart of ill health and compromised performance. This book is written in a style that is as if you were having a conversation with Dr. Schoen. He brilliantly explains much of the current scientific research in ways that a non-scientist can understand."

—Larry Drell, M.D., medical director, Anxiety and Depression Therapy Services, Washington, DC

"Dr. Schoen does a great job of using real patient stories to show how our mind and body are inseparable. Through his insights, readers will better understand how our reactions to life's challenges can trigger some of our most challenging health problems. They will also gain some valuable tools for combating their complex medical issues."

—Steven Tan, M.D., UCLA clinical professor of medicine

"In a world with more creature comforts, we see more impatience, discomfort, anxiety, and depression. In a world that provides us tools for connection, the paradox is that we are technologically hyper-connected yet disconnected from ourselves. What is the effect of being on alert constantly—handling a barrage of e-mails, texts, and a never ending to-do list? In *Your Survival Instinct Is Killing You*, Dr. Marc Schoen reveals the effects of living in a constant state of fight or flight and details the toll that this lifestyle is taking on our health. Fortunately, Dr. Schoen also provides brilliant insights and practical tools on how to counteract the effects of these twenty-first-century stressors. This is a must-read for anyone who is overwhelmed with the demands of modern life and needs a way out before it's too late—in effect, this is a must-read for everyone!"

—Dr. Patricia Fitzgerald, D.A.O.M., L.Ac., C.C.N., doctor of acupuncture and Oriental medicine; medical director, Santa Monica Wellness Center; author, *The Detox Solution*; health editor, *The Huffington Post*

Your Survival Instinct Is Killing You

Retrain Your Brain to Conquer Fear, Make Better Decisions, and Thrive in the 21st Century

Marc Schoen, Ph.D.
with Kristin Loberg

HUDSON STREET PRESS

HUDSON STREET PRESS
Published by the Penguin Group
Penguin Group (USA) Inc., 375 Hudson Street,
New York, New York 10014, USA

USA | Canada | UK | Ireland | Australia | New Zealand | India | South Africa | China
Penguin Books Ltd, Registered Offices: 80 Strand, London WC2R 0RL, England
For more information about the Penguin Group visit penguin.com

First published by Hudson Street Press, a member of Penguin Group (USA) Inc., 2013

LIBRARY OF CONGRESS CATALOGING-IN-PUBLICATION DATA
Schoen, Marc.
Your survival instinct is killing you : retrain your brain to conquer fear, make better decisions, and thrive in the 21st century / Marc Schoen with Kristin Loberg.
p. cm.
Includes bibliographical references and index.
ISBN 978-1-59463-097-2 (hardcover)
1. Instinct. 2. Mind and body. 3. Decision making. 4. Intuition. I. Loberg, Kristin. II. Title.
BF685.S28 2013
155.9—dc23 2012037843

Printed in the United States of America
10 9 8 7 6 5 4 3 2 1

Set in Warnock Pro with Abadi Mt Std
Designed by Daniel Lagin

PUBLISHER'S NOTE
While the authors have made every effort to provide accurate telephone numbers, Internet addresses, and other contact information at the time of publication, neither the publisher nor the authors assume any responsibility for errors or for changes that occur after publication. Further, publisher does not have any control over and does not assume any responsibility for author or third-party Web sites or their content.

This book is dedicated to my mother and father
for their love and for always believing in me.

This book is also dedicated to all of my patients
through the years who have allowed me to serve them,
and learn and grow along with them.

It is not the strongest of the species that survives, nor the most intelligent that survives. It is the one that is the most adaptable to change.

—Charles Darwin

Contents

Part 1

The Nature of Discomfort

Chapter 1

The 21st-Century Survivalist

The New Paradigm for Transforming Discomfort into Power

Have you ever stopped to marvel at how clever your body really is?

In just the past second, trillions of cellular transactions took place within you—but you didn't have to direct even one percent of them. And at the same time, each of those cells was given the proper nourishment to replenish its activity. You didn't need to consciously do one thing. Yes, the mind and body are unbelievably capable of sustaining our lives and the status quo. But what happens when the status quo is no longer supporting our health and our behavior in a productive way?

Take, for example, the sixty-year-old man with intractable hiccups who was admitted at the hospital where I was working early in my career as a psychologist. Despite my specialization in hypnosis and my understanding how valuable it could be to some medical conditions at the time, my work was relegated to traditional psychology—treating patients who were depressed, suicidal, schizophrenic, or had multiple personalities. I was not supposed to roam the medical units of the hospital. But on this particular day, unbeknownst to me, a battle had commenced related to this patient.

His name was Mikael and he had been suffering from hiccups for more than two years. The hiccups had gotten so bad that they were now causing seizures. After the doctors had tried everything at their disposal, they now wanted to perform a craniotomy (open up his brain) and sever a nerve to interrupt the hiccup reflex. As you can imagine, the family was not happy about this idea, and desperately searched for other solutions.

One of the man's children knew that hypnosis had been documented in the past to resolve this condition, and through his research also had learned that I was the only staff member at the hospital who could conduct hypnosis. The family then pursued this option through the primary physician involved with the case, asking that I be allowed to have a consultation with their father. Their request was flatly rejected, and the family followed up by raising the issue to the medical staff and hospital administration. Again, they were turned down on the grounds that hypnosis was unscientific, not medically necessary, and unproven. Not until relentless pleas from the family did the hospital finally acquiesce and permit my involvement.

At just twenty-nine years old, and one of the youngest members on staff, I was thrilled to finally have an opportunity to apply my skills to medical conditions beyond those saved for psychiatry. I had no idea that so much conflict and resistance had preceded my invitation to visit this patient, but when I stepped into Mikael's private room, I was shocked to see the walls lined with physicians, hospital administrators, and family members. Clearly, my work and I were on trial as I faced a very unsupportive and unfriendly group that misunderstood my methods and probably thought I was about to conduct some quasi-magical procedure that reeked of quackery. The tension in the room was palpable, and I hoped that just this once performance anxiety would not be paying me a visit.

I approached the patient and initiated a conversation. He was hiccupping nearly every fifteen to twenty seconds. But to make matters worse, he spoke only broken English. I remember thinking, "Just great. I finally get my big break, but it's with someone who may not even be able to communicate or understand me. With a room full of people looking for me to fail, couldn't my first test be something a little less challenging?" I proceeded, and began to engage in a broken conversation with Mikael, quickly learning that he came from the northern reaches of Finland. His hand was cold when I shook it, and I joked with him that this hospital room probably felt familiar since he had experience living in a cold climate. He smiled slightly, and then I noticed that his hiccups halted briefly as I alluded to the coolness. I wondered if there was a connection, so I decided to develop this interaction further.

I began to talk much more in-depth about coolness, while bringing in my hypnotic skills and slowing my voice somewhat. His hiccups became less and less frequent. I thought that if I could help him experience another physical sensation in his body, this new sensation could compete with and block the hiccup reflex. Emboldened, I continued to talk to him about snow, and how sometimes we can get so cold that it's hard to feel anything else. Even our chest gets cold—so cold, in fact, that we just want to stop, rest, and do nothing else. Within ten minutes, Mikael's hiccups had vanished. They never returned. When I left the room, everyone (including me) was stunned that a chronic condition scheduled for brain surgery was resolved in just ten minutes of talking. The year was 1983, just as mind-body medicine was beginning to gain recognition, slowly and sporadically, throughout the traditional medical community.

It sometimes takes a dramatic event like this to change dated assumptions about biology and open oneself up to a new perspective on how we function and how the body can, with the help of simple mind-body techniques, snap itself out of a cycle that perpetuates disease or dysfunction. Although I tapped my hypnosis skills to create an enduring shift in this particular patient, the principles behind the change had application in a much broader way. My work with Mikael made it very evident to me how the body becomes imprisoned within a groove and cannot break free from its grip. It becomes habituated to repeatedly react a certain way, like a broken record. By teaching the body to experience new sensations, it can forge new and more productive neural networks so that it may find a path to wellness.

Although we didn't have the technology then, we know now from current research that these new experiences create new road maps in the brain. It's like changing a recipe: With the altering of an ingredient, a different result emerges. Although I used hypnosis to elicit the change in Mikael, in the thirty years since, I have learned there are simpler and more practical means of accomplishing the same goal. The secret, of course, is determining the best method to encourage the brain and body to accept and embrace new knowledge.

Eradicating Mikael's hiccups at this state-of-the-art hospital marked a turning point in my career. No longer would I—or any of my psychologist colleagues—be discouraged from entering the medical unit with our "nontraditional" methods of treatment. I began performing mind-body techniques on patients, and was able to go as far as to conduct hypnosis throughout the hospital. In fact, soon thereafter I founded and became the director of the hospital's Psychoimmune Program, one of the first of its kind in the country, and started educating residents and fellows from all areas of medicine about the psychodynamics of sickness, or how the mind influences health.

So what was it that led to Mikael's endless loop of hiccups? Many persistent symptoms, in fact, can start innocently enough but go on relentlessly—a cold that leads to a lingering cough; a stomach bug that leaves you with a long-term aversion to the food you ate just before getting sick; or a sports injury in which the pain continues after it's allegedly healed, and there's no pathology to support it. But once the initial cause of these symptoms passes, there is a new spark that fuels them. And for many people, the spark is a rising level of what I am going to label as "discomfort"—a discomfort that creates a new network in the brain and body that continually feeds the symptoms. Amazingly, this level of discomfort flies below their mental radar until a symptom crescendos and takes root.

This was precisely the case with Mikael, who, after several years of poorly managed discomfort, found himself saddled with near-constant hiccups and an impending craniotomy. I later learned that prior to his bout with hiccups, he had experienced significant losses in his life. For some individuals, hiccups can be a reaction to being upset or fearful. And for almost everyone, they resolve relatively quickly. But in Mikael's case they didn't, and his level of angst continued to feed them, pressing them into a brain pattern and eventually turning them into a cyclical spiral of misery capable of inducing seizures.

I've worked with thousands of people whose health, happiness, and decision making have been compromised by discomfort and fear, which has enslaved them in behavioral patterns that are unproductive and unfulfilling. I've helped chronic migraine and headache sufferers who are struck with pain when exposed to fluorescent lights, air conditioning, or a deadline by teaching them how to stop being physically affected by these triggers. I've helped numerous people break the cycle of suffering attacks whenever they encounter certain situations, such as a freeway overpass, an elevator, or a stuffy room full of people. One of the universal experiences I routinely see is what I call the Let Down Effect, which transpires when a person always gets sick over the holidays, while on vacation, or after a big deadline has been met. I've also assisted the time-crunched and harassed CEO who functions well most of the time but becomes seriously unraveled when making decisions under pressure. None of these simple cause-and-effect relationships are arbitrary. They are dynamic manifestations of the body's neurobiological wiring that science can now explain, and they have far-reaching ramifications for how we stay healthy and even how we age.

Misbehaving Instincts

Most people wrongly assume that a clinical psychologist like me would deal with purely emotional issues and mental illness. This couldn't be further from the truth. Today the majority of my work entails teaching people how to change their mind and body's reactions to internal and external influences that can perpetuate chronic health conditions and other annoying and lingering symptoms. A bad case of the hiccups pales in comparison to other health problems that can result from a similar chain of reactions in a body whose cellular transmissions have veered wildly off track. In fact, the hiccup scenario serves as a great example for understanding myriad conditions that besiege millions today, including insomnia, poor decision-making skills under pressure, obesity, chronic pain, arthritis, panic and anxiety disorders, depression, headaches, chronic fatigue, allergies, irritable bowel and other gastrointestinal problems, and skin disorders such as acne and eczema. So yes, my practice may be different from that of medical doctors, but one thing we all witness is the growing number of patients suffering from these and other chronic conditions.

Such problems may seem vastly different, but they often have a single common denominator that has gone virtually unnoticed: a misbehaving survival instinct. In many cases, disease processes and compromised behavioral patterns are not solely rooted in the body, but they are also stitched deep within the most primitive area of our brain—the limbic system, the place where many of our ancient physical and behavioral reactions are encoded, setting the course of our behavior, health, and wellness. It is also the place where, working with my patients, I attempt to stimulate the production of new neuronal pathways that ultimately redirect the body's biological path away from illness and misfiring to one that fosters health and productive behavioral patterns.

MEET THE SURVIVAL INSTINCT

I'm going to show you how this very fundamental part of us—our survival instinct—either underlies and exacerbates many conditions or contributes to their chronic nature. By learning how to control this critical mechanism with my approach, people can manage and in some cases totally eradicate these maladies in a relatively short time period—often *without drugs*. Just as I snapped Mikael's body out of a dangerous hiccup loop, you, too, can learn how to extricate yourself from old instinctual patterns that are paralyzing and undermining the quality of your life. I'll teach you how, with methods I honed helping thousands of patients.

In essence, this book, which describes these practical methods, is an exploration of our survival instinct's extraordinary powers and the ways in which you, too, can benefit from my approach and optimize your own well-being. Even if you don't live with a chronic condition, this book will help you to create a healthy response to the world. Indeed, you can now stop feeling trapped on a treadmill in which your physical health and body are managing you, and can instead take hold of the controls and find new and healthy outcomes. With this book you're also going to learn how you can liberate yourself from fears and frustrations that keep you from functioning at your very best both at work and at home. Imagine, if you will, that you can achieve more peace and less struggle in your life than you have ever known. That is my wish for you, and it's closer than you might think.

My guess is you've never experienced a bout with hiccups as bad as Mikael's, but by virtue of being human, you've certainly had your fair share of unwanted behaviors and symptoms. Perhaps you're the insomniac who hasn't had a good night's sleep in years. Or you're a time-pressed executive who is looking to enhance your ability to make successful business decisions under pressure. Maybe you've battled with your weight because you cannot stop overeating. Or perhaps you're simply sick and tired of being sick and tired, constantly struggling to find more authentic energy and a sense of peaceful well-being.

At the heart of this book is the connection between our tolerance for discomfort and its link to our inborn survival instincts, which play a huge role in our neurobiological wiring. Recent advances in science show that these instantaneous survivalist reactions have far-reaching ramifications for how we stay healthy, how we behave and perform, how we handle adversity, how we make decisions, and how we weather the passage of time. Much of our body—all the way down to our cells and their biochemistry—can fall into patterns dictated by our survival instinct that are potentially destructive to our long-term health.

Your survival instinct is working inside you right now. It's that programmed part of you that controls what to do intuitively to save yourself when necessary, such as get up and run out of a burning building. Rarely do you need to recruit this part of you today, because you seldom find yourself in situations that are truly life threatening. Yet I witness this instinct in action daily among patients whose chronic conditions have come to define their lives. It's the culprit acting up in the person who cannot stop overeating, the insomniac who can't find sleep, the executive who cannot gain control of his panic attacks when he prepares for a big meeting, and the individual who cannot open herself up to love because of past heartache. In all of these cases, their hair-trigger survival instinct is being unnecessarily pressed into action at the slightest hint of discomfort, manifesting itself in these injurious and destructive behaviors. Once the survival instinct seizes control of the body, it gains the power to perpetuate illness and disease and undermine decisions and focus, without people even knowing it.

I'm compelled to write this book because I work in a mainstream medical system in which the region of the mind where our survival instinct hides is only partially understood. Even today, our instincts don't receive the total respect that they warrant. All too often, scientific data that clearly links our survival instinct with ill health, chronic disease, and accelerated aging is grossly overlooked. Over the past thirty years, I've been working in the trenches of demystifying how the mind influences physical health—gaining an enormous body of knowledge from the one-on-one work I do with individuals. I was among the first scientists to introduce to the medical community how mind-body tools such as hypnosis could be used to influence physical reactions such as inflammation in the body, and I started training medical students, interns, residents, and fellows from all areas of medicine in the mind's role in influencing illness and health more than twenty-five years ago.

Today, I continue to study and teach mind-body medicine as well as design programs for my patients to remedy a wide spectrum of health challenges and disorders. I help hundreds of patients, from pro athletes to stay-at-home parents, manage (and in many cases totally eliminate) unrelenting stress, daily headaches, serial colds, embarrassing skin disorders, food obsessions, life-disrupting panic attacks, chronic pain, arthritis, and more. But I know that my reach is limited to my practice and local community. My hope and wish is that this book allows me to reach a larger segment of the population that does not have these resources immediately available, and to provide a means of creating lasting change. So if you're among the millions who suffer from chronic symptoms or health challenges that haven't been eradicated by traditional medicine, my hope is that this book will help you to find relief at last. The time has come for you to examine how you cope with discomfort in your life, how it affects your inborn survival instinct, and how you can make slight shifts in your lifestyle to support optimal health and well-being.

The Sinking Threshold

Paradoxically, as the comfort in our lives has expanded thanks to technology, the presence of our survival instinct in action is at an all-time high in our lives and culture. Rather than lessening, our intolerance for discomfort is on an upswing, instilling within us an increasingly lower "discomfort threshold" and setting us up to be more and more at the mercy of our primitive instincts and reactions that can perpetuate disease and dysfunction.

The good news is that there is much we can do to reset this threshold. Although our ancestral instincts direct us to flee even the anticipation of discomfort, it is now possible to transform these instincts to accept a greater tolerance for discomfort while embracing a far greater level of safety. There is little chance that we can ever fully avoid being uncomfortable, for it will always be part of our experience as humans. You will learn in this book that your overall level of comfort is often predicated on your tolerance of discomfort, and that you can build up your "instinctual muscles" for successfully managing discomfort while turning down your overly reactive survival instinct.

The topics covered in this book are wide ranging; whether you suffer from chronic pain, unraveling under pressure, or a chronic addiction to the cookie jar late at night, you will find relevant information and strategies pertinent to you. Along the way, I will push you to embrace a new perspective on health and abandon a few conventional wisdoms. I'll also be answering an array of questions you likely never thought to ask, such as:

- Can compulsively checking e-mail and texts fuel a toxic reaction in our body?
- Can relaxation be hazardous to our health?
- Can the survival instinct be a major cause of today's epidemic challenges with overeating and substance abuse?
- Can we blame chronic conditions such as insomnia, anxiety disorders, and a growing number of pain conditions on our survival instinct?
- Can our inherent need to feel safe be the ultimate driver of health and wellness?

The answer to all of these questions is a resounding yes, as I will show. Many of my patients come to me after they've become entrapped within a pattern of avoidance and fear, medication regimens, and a powerlessness to control their health, and are at the mercy of their condition. Working with me, however, they can acquire the tools to manage and prevent future episodes. They learn how to tame their survival instinct so it doesn't get in the way of living to their fullest potential. My hope is that you will recover, too, using the methods described in this book.

Contrary to some other books, which target a specific problem such as weight or sleep, I'm dealing here with an array of possible issues that all share one common characteristic: an overly sensitive survival instinct. The focus in this book is on that shared element rather than the myriad resulting conditions. Thus, this book will unfold chapter by chapter, starting with a broad discussion about discomfort and its roots, and its relationship to the survival instinct. Then you're going to learn what living up to the rigors of modern life could be doing to you from a behavioral and biochemical standpoint.

This is hardly an arbitrary discussion: To satisfy the skeptics and scientifically minded readers, I will discuss and review the accumulating evidence that shows how features of contemporary culture are progressively altering our physiology right down to the most primitive regions of our brains, where our survival instinct holds the keys to the kingdom of our health and happiness. This discussion examines a spectrum of forces, such as a sizable increase in the importance we place on our external world, our growing reliance on powerful technologies that compels us to stay plugged in, and our escalating need to be instantly gratified. When you add those trends together, you have an exponential outcome that can incite the survivalist in anyone. The world neither looks nor feels safe anymore. And your instincts know it.

For readers who don't care to understand the science behind all this, you'll find plenty of embedded stories and practical strategies to apply to your own life and keep you learning even when you don't realize it. Just having a general understanding of how your survival instinct works inside you every day will be enough to make an enduring and profound positive impact on your life. (I also invite you to check out my website at www.marcschoen.com to access additional material that complements this book's lessons. There, you'll be able to download files to further personalize the techniques described in this book, as well as benefit from using supplemental exercises that only the Internet's technology can provide.)

After taking you on a tour of exactly what happens inside the body when your survival instinct turns on and remains on, I'll show you how to retrain this instinct. Don't panic: This won't entail any crazy recommendations to see a neurosurgeon or just chant "things will be okay" to yourself the next time you feel anxious and edgy. The practical tools and techniques I'll be giving you are easier to master than you think, and anyone can do it. And they can be applied to virtually any type of behavior, whether you wrestle with a phobia, stress, or a health condition, or you just can't find a way to relax on weekends and avoid work or responding to e-mail. I wonder if you'll find glimpses of your own personal struggles as you explore the numerous case studies and anecdotes, and as you discover novel solutions and tools to create meaningful changes in your life.

Obviously, we cannot cease the march of time and the progression of society, but we can learn how to adapt healthfully to most circumstances and keep our survival instinct in check. Indeed, adaptation is the hallmark of our human existence. The upcoming century very well could be all about learning to thrive with less comfort as our society undergoes inevitable transitions in all facets of our livelihood. Those individuals who can master this new survival skill will most likely have the greatest opportunity to create abundance in all areas of their life: social, work, and health. Put simply, you're going to learn how to transform discomfort into power. By learning how to harness discomfort, you can improve your life right down to the decisions you make every day and that have a lasting impact. Let this book guide you through developing new, required skills so that a secure, healthy, and successful future is within your reach. This book is, at its heart, a modern guide to survival.

Chapter 2

The Cozy Paradox

Uncomfortable in a Comfortable World

Several years ago I received a call from a patient named James, whom I hadn't seen for twenty years. He'd originally sought help in managing the stress he was experiencing while studying for the California bar exam, and later the Louisiana bar exam. Not long after he passed his tests, he moved to New Orleans to settle down and practice law. Like other patients I've seen through the years who return for a visit to Los Angeles, James contacted me after all that time to say hello again and bring me up to date. He also wanted to seek my opinion related to his ailing parent.

James had grown up in a rural setting, so I was curious about how he had adjusted to living in a busy city that is constantly bustling with activities and nightlife. On the surface he was living the life he dreamed, and wished he had moved to New Orleans sooner.

"I've never felt better," he declared.

Later in the conversation James began to yawn and then rub his forehead. I asked him if he was feeling all right. He mentioned that he had slept poorly the night before, and had awakened with a headache. What followed was a shift from our casual and getting reacquainted conversation to one of more seriousness. I asked him how well he slept in general and how often he had these headaches. James seemed surprised by my sudden concern about his health.

"I think I generally sleep fine," he said. "But last night I had to use a sleeping pill."

I then asked him how often and how long he had been taking sleeping pills. That's when he said matter-of-factly, "Well, it began last year when I started having these terrible headaches."

"Have you been evaluated by a physician for these conditions?" I asked.

"Oh yes. He's the one that gave me the sleeping pills!"

As it turned out, his doctor had diagnosed him with cluster headaches and felt that his nerves and poor sleep were probably to blame. He'd been prescribed Ativan for his nerves and as a sleep aid. He'd also been given barbiturate-based Fiorinal with codeine to help him manage his headaches. James wasn't totally sold on the idea, but he nevertheless used the prescribed medication regularly. When I asked him more questions about his bedtime routine, he described how he typically became anxious about the mere thought of going to bed, worrying that he wouldn't be able to fall asleep, and that if he didn't get the sleep he needed, he was destined to develop a headache. So it didn't take long for his sleep medication to become a normal part of his bedtime habit as well. And, he told me, although he used to wait to see if he'd run into difficulties with falling asleep, now he found himself downing an Ativan every night no matter what.

"And what about the headache medication? How often do you take that?" I asked.

"I have learned to take it at the slightest hint of a headache in order to head it off before it turns into something big," James replied. "It can be after breakfast, if I am uncomfortable, and sometimes at bedtime." As if it was no big deal.

As with the sleep aids, James used to wait on taking the pain pills but now took them at the slightest hint of discomfort. And since he saw stress as the culprit, he was finding himself at times taking Ativan during the day, particularly before an important meeting. James was now living in a cycle of pill popping that acted as a preemptive strike against his fears and ailments.

My concern must have been evident to James from my facial expressions alone. He said, "I admit I'm not happy about this either. But I think this just goes with the territory as we get busier, older, and have more responsibilities," he stated.

But I wasn't reassured by James, and I was reluctant to accept that his experience reflected the natural course of aging. Much to the contrary, I felt deeply troubled, for I also noticed that James had gained a lot of weight since I had last seen him. Although he was doing his best to present a strong front, I could see that he was losing ground to an insidious undertow.

What James described to me that day is not an outlier case of someone who lacks good sleep habits and healthy coping skills to combat stress and anxiety. I knew too well that what he characterized so perfectly is a problem that is taking hold in pandemic proportions across America and likely other parts of the world. In the past decade or so, I've observed a burgeoning pattern among the hundreds of patients I treat, despite their unique issues. It's a pattern that reflects a most peculiar phenomenon that is prevalent in our culture today. Theoretically, those of us living in the developed world are a lot safer now than ever before. We don't have to worry so much about dying of infectious disease, medical advancements have lengthened the average life span by several decades, crime is relatively low, and in America we haven't seen civil war in nearly 150 years. And we have access to an enormous number of conveniences to make life easier, from the Internet and other technologies to plentiful food supplies and inexpensive means of traveling. But we've also grown increasingly less tolerant of being uncomfortable, and our threshold for discomfort is rapidly shrinking. At the mere hint of being uncomfortable, there is an urgent need to take action to relieve or end it. And if it is not managed expediently, then there is an escalating fear that we won't be able to cope, or that something horrific will unfold.

The proof is easy to spot; it's in our growing reliance on pharmaceuticals such as antidepressants, painkillers, sleep aids, and ADHD and antianxiety drugs; our rising emotional discord that results in behavioral and emotional overreactions, from overeating to road rage; and a general sense that we're all living on the verge of a temper tantrum. This widespread unease has even affected our children, more than a quarter of whom now take a medication on a chronic basis.

Think about your own life. Does your temper get triggered easily by inconsequential events such as when someone cuts in front of you in line or when navigating through an automated telephone service? Do you ever feel pain somewhere and immediately worry that a catastrophic illness like cancer is to blame? Do you ever seek food the moment you feel any degree of hunger or unease? Do you sometimes feel like you're living on the brink of a meltdown, constantly thinking about your next e-mail, text message, or your unending to-do list? It's as if we're feeling suffocated in a world where we shouldn't feel that way. Despite an enormous array of goods and services to make us feel happy, comfortable, and safe, we're rarely content, and any hint of struggle quickly causes us to feel physically and emotionally threatened. The end result is that we're more inclined to develop symptoms and illnesses as we scramble to cope with our growing intolerance of discomfort. We're more at risk for addictions and serious relationship dysfunction. We are, put simply, not comfortable in a world that is increasingly designed for comfort—where we expect to be cozy, healthy, and happy all the time.

The more I noticed this prevailing phenomenon over years of working with patients and seminar participants, the more I sought clear answers. Why have we lost the ability to deal with any adversity? Why is it that in the absence of serious threats—famine, war, pestilence, the proverbial saber-toothed tiger—we wage these wars within us? Why does our internal comfort zone feel cramped when we have wonderful advancements at hand to make life easier and, in a lot of ways, *better*? It's astonishing to think that depression, for example, is the leading cause of disability worldwide as measured by "YLD"—Years Lost due to Disability—a metric used by the World Health Organization to refer to how many healthy years are lost due to a health condition. In many developed countries, such as the United States, depression is already among the top causes of both disability and premature death. Why are we so depressed when we have fewer things to be depressed about?

When you look around you, you can see that the depth of people's fears today is much greater than it was just twenty years ago. It's what I call the Cozy Paradox: Despite the growing ubiquity of comfort in our lives, we have become increasingly oversensitive to discomfort—so much so that even subtle adversity and general uneasiness have become capable of inculcating fear and unsettling our physical and emotional health. As you'll learn shortly, disturbing external influences lie at the center of this Cozy Paradox. They can be any number of things, ranging from fluorescent lighting that triggers migraines to calls from your boss that stir agitated feelings leading to sheer panic. In James's case, the Cozy Paradox is the fact that he lives in one of the most enthralling cities in the world yet harbors fears of insomnia and has to medicate himself to get through his day successfully. He may not describe himself as "uncomfortable," but it's the best word to describe his predicament, which is emblematic of how millions of people live today.

What's important to understand is that our belief about doing well and that we are in control is often belied by our body screaming to the contrary, with symptoms that rage increasingly more out of control. It's as if we're living in a house with a leaky roof and are constantly trying to contain the leaks. We are busy doing patchwork on our leaky body with medications, medical procedures, and external distractions, on which we have become increasingly reliant. Clients like James are a common segment of my practice—they appear fine on the surface, but an entirely different picture of them unfolds as they talk about their physical symptoms, daily medications, how much stress they bear, and to what extent they feel in control of their life.

It's also important to emphasize that in most cases, people like James are not deliberately lying to themselves or others. The mind has an extraordinary ability to overlook, minimize, and even detach from physical and psychological symptoms that have developed. Perhaps this is what has made us such an adaptable species. For centuries, humans have been able to adjust to extreme living conditions—whether it's the deep freezes of Alaska or the searing temperatures of the Sahara desert. This quality of adaptation no doubt has many great benefits. On the other hand, it can lead us to keep our heads in the sand and not notice that symptoms are beginning to escalate that can significantly alter our lives, driving us, for instance, to live in more restricted ways. James reached the point where he didn't think he'd be able to sleep without his medication, or get through his workday without having his antianxiety drugs on hand. While he may not have thought he was living a restricted lifestyle, his reliance on such crutches defined his limitations. Symptoms and reactions can develop below the radar, and it's not until people's attention is alerted to them or their symptoms begin to commandeer their life that they realize the magnitude of their predicament. I don't think James tuned in to his own plight until our meeting that day. I assured him, however, that his experience reflected the goings-on in society at large. His story also gave me great pause.

We live in one of the greatest nations on earth, with access to the world's best medicine and knowledge, and despite spending more money per person on health care than any other country, the United States lags embarrassingly behind in terms of population health. We rank fourteenth among the nations that have the lowest percentage of preventable deaths; we rank twenty-fourth in terms of life expectancy. And on the happiness scale, we don't even make the top twenty; we come in at twenty-three. (Denmark claims to have the happiest people on the planet.) So despite increasing access to things that make life easier and more comfortable, our happiness quotient is hardly being boosted.

How is it that in our advanced technological era, symptoms and conditions such as obesity, depression, panic and anxiety disorders, sleeplessness, autoimmune disorders, allergies, chronic pain, heart disease, gastrointestinal problems, certain cancers, and fatigue are more rampant than ever? Doesn't this seem paradoxical? Treatment for such conditions is not stemming the tide. Have we overlooked an important element? What's missing?

The answer to that question entails a more in-depth understanding and appreciation of the role that discomfort plays in our life and its relationship to our survival instinct. It lies at the heart of our health and abundance in the unfolding twenty-first century.

Feeding the Discomfort

Perhaps there's no better way to understand the origins of discomfort and its potential behavioral consequences than to hear a few stories of people who illustrate this phenomenon well. James's story demonstrates the effects of trying to deal with discomfort in ways that may not actually be benefiting his overall health. Now let's take a closer look at how this discomfort can manifest in other ways. I'll start with one of my patients, whom I'll call Kate, who reflects the millions of people struggling to cope with their weight.

Kate was about to start another diet when she came to see me at the request of her primary-care physician, who worried she was prediabetic. She was like many other patients I'd treated in her condition—overweight for far too long and seeking an end to the frustration and anguish of failing again and again at weight loss. The thought of diabetes was terrifying, and her doctor was concerned that, given her history with diets, another attempt at classic dieting using a self-help program or a commercial weight loss program wouldn't solve the problem. For Kate, the weight started to come on during her college days, when the freshman twenty became a permanent fixture. Now she felt like there was no hope of turning off her "voracious eating machine," as she called it. And like so many others in her situation, she was well versed in all the popular ideas circling the field today—good carbs versus bad carbs, the perils of processed foods, and the bane of emotional, recreational, and mindless eating. Group therapy had trimmed a few inches here and there, but she always wound up back where she'd started. Kate had embarked on a rigorous exercise program thinking that getting into shape would somehow also change her eating habits. And she had also experimented with medically supervised weight loss that included many different diet pills meant to stimulate her metabolism, squelch her appetite, and make fatty foods unappealing. Suffice it to say Kate won the gold medal for effort, but she hadn't found the thinner, healthier version of herself.

After I let Kate chronicle her journey, I asked her a simple question: "How often do you eat when you're actually hungry?" She admitted that she was seldom hungry but found herself eating regardless. According to Kate, she was "hardwired" to eat uncontrollably. It didn't matter what emotion she was feeling, either. She found herself eating whether she was bored, happy, apathetic, or sad. I agreed that there was something to be said for our thoughts and emotions affecting our eating behaviors, but I also suggested that our inner *instincts* had something to do with it—in a big way, and especially for someone like Kate. I asked, "What happens when you want to eat but try *not* to? Do you *really* begin to feel hungrier?"

Now, this question stumped Kate, and caused her to reconsider her well-rehearsed and pat responses. When she really thought about it, she admitted that she didn't necessarily feel any hungrier when she tried to avoid eating.

"So then why do you feel you need to eat?" I asked.

Instead of hunger, what she felt was a general uneasiness—a sense of being physically uncomfortable, which she described using the words *restless*, *antsy*, and *edgy*. This would then precipitate her need to eat, because food eased these sensations.

Acknowledging this discomfort was a huge step for Kate, even though she was just beginning to understand its role in her life. I went on to help her come to terms with it by sharing the difference between two distinct parts of her brain that relate to eating. I explained that the oldest part of our brain experiences the perceived lack of food or the anticipation of scarcity as a danger signal; it's wired to take action in an instinctual manner whenever it feels it's in harm's way. And when this survival instinct's button is pushed, our ancient hardwiring focuses on whatever it needs to do to assure our survival. So it seizes control of our logical mind and takes over our whole body.

As you probably know, long ago we were hardwired to survive by consuming food, especially if we didn't know when we will eat again. One way to get sustenance quickly was to consume calorie-dense foods, and ever since, this instinctive behavior has been stitched within us. Our early ancestors didn't need to worry about gaining weight; these preprogrammed instructions to load up on these types of foods had survival value. Look no further than your pet dog to understand these instincts. Dogs don't lounge through their meals. Instead, they gulp them down as if they are fearful the food will be taken away. They are in fact driven by the instinct that this meal could be their last, even though they are consistently fed.

After Kate took a few moments to digest what I was telling her, she asked an obvious question: "Are you saying that I'm eating to satisfy my survival instincts? That doesn't make sense to me. Shouldn't my instincts be driving someone like me to eat less?"

I agreed that this would make logical sense, but the problem is that this part of the brain is not concerned with logic or healthy beliefs or thoughts. It's instead driven by old programmed instincts honed eons ago, when food wasn't so plentiful and eating served the sole purpose of preserving our species. But now, this instinct is no longer necessary, yet it operates as if it is. I also explained to Kate that traditional weight loss treatments for overeaters emphasize the importance of correcting thought patterns related to food, such as "this is not healthy," or "these are empty calories," or "this will make you fat." But often these components are only a small part of the big picture, and are trying to tame the often feisty and independent-minded survival instinct that is actually driving the eating behavior. Unfortunately, these thought and belief approaches often fail to penetrate and influence our limbic brain, leaving the survival instinct in full control of our overeating behavior.

Of course, Kate next asked about how she could change her programmed behavior and teach herself to eat less despite such a powerful underlying force.

"You need to become more comfortable with being *uncomfortable.* Going on another regimented diet won't take the survival instinct's needs away, and it will continue to drive your eating behavior. And in many cases, the survival instinct will undermine the results of whatever you do, even if you one day consider something drastic like surgery. So you will need to work on training that primitive part of your brain to no longer equate being uncomfortable with danger or being unsafe—especially when you face no real danger. And by doing so, you'll find yourself turning to food less and less."

Given this explanation, I made a deal with Kate: I encouraged her to test, on a short-term basis, what would happen to her when her survival instinct was retrained, rather than rush immediately into another diet or sign up for a formal program. She accepted the challenge, and we went to work on taming this inner part that would always be with her. To Kate's astonishment, she began to lose weight relatively quickly and ultimately found—for the first time—that she could sustain a significant weight loss. She also steered her blood sugars down to a healthy range, reducing her risk for becoming diabetic.

Kate managed to gain control of her weight within a year of work with me, which reflected nearly the same results she could have expected from any traditional diet. But she achieved so much more than control over her weight, bonuses that another diet could not have provided. Kate could now sustain her weight loss long-term. She also applied the same lessons and strategies she learned with me in her effort to lose weight to a variety of other challenges in her life. Having a survival instinct in shape for the twenty-first century made all the difference. She began to experience more fulfilling relationships, weathered stress and adversity better, became more effective and productive at work, and achieved an improvement in her well-being that even impressed her doctor.

Contrary to what you might think, Kate's dramatic changes were not the result of willpower and personal restraint courtesy of a regimented program. They were a direct outcome of coming to terms with the core cause of her overeating, which had nothing to do with physical hunger and had everything to do with a neglected part of her brain that ached to be safe and sound.

The 21st-Century Escape Artist

Make no mistake, our survival instinct is affecting and influencing a growing number of facets in our twenty-first-century lives. Most everyone is familiar with the fight-or-flight reaction. We'd run away from a charging bull or pick up a weapon to duke it out. The survivalist in all of us is incredibly powerful—and convincing. It's that programmed soldier born with us who tells us what to do intuitively to save ourselves when necessary. Rarely do we need to recruit this inborn warrior today because rarely do we find ourselves in situations that are truly life threatening. But the fight-or-flight reaction, which is powered by the survival instinct, is becoming more and more prevalent, while genuine life-threatening danger becomes less so. And as petty situations increasingly trigger our survival instinct, we find our comfort zone shrinking. Eventually, we feel imprisoned by a narrower and finite space, which only increases our feelings of vulnerability.

As I explained in detail to Kate, our inner survivalist lives in the farthest reaches of the brain, in the limbic system, which formed after humans began evolving from reptiles. Its instincts have deep, permanent connections to visceral, or automatic, responses. It's the part of us that we share with much of the animal kingdom, and it is the home of our primary emotions such as fear, pleasure, love, lust, pain, and rage. It's also the seat of our addictions, as well as sensations of safety, hunger, and thirst. In fact, virtually all of our gut responses originate in this ancient part of the brain. These responses are also very trainable. By "trainable,"

I'm referring to the fact they are easily capable of becoming associated with certain circumstances, which can then influence our behavior, thoughts, and emotions. If, for example, you have a panic attack in an elevator, you may find yourself inadvertently conditioned or trained to have a panic attack in future elevator encounters.

Clearly, many of our body's knee-jerk reactions help us to survive in our world, but when those reactions lead to illness or injury, this powerful system has essentially gone awry. Like an Olympic swimmer who trains his body to reflexively flip around when he approaches the wall at the end of the pool, we can train ourselves to respond automatically to external conditions, essentially becoming "programmed" to know when, what, and how much to eat; when to sleep; when to feel ill, healthy, or happy; what is fun and sexy; and so on.

So many of today's maladies are driven by this primitive brain, which, as we'll learn in chapter 5, is the ultimate creator of habits. As I also explained to Kate, this is why cognitive approaches, or what I call "lecturing the emotions," can fail to improve matters. They rely too much on the cerebral brain, and in particular the cerebral cortex—the modern, advanced section of the human brain—to be the purveyor of change, while our instincts and intense emotions stored below in the limbic brain remain untouched and unaddressed. As you might have guessed already, the limbic and cerebral brain speak two vastly different languages, just as two people living under the same roof can possess two different personalities and rely on separate forms of communication. The cerebral brain is reflecting, calculating, and logical; it prefers to engage in critical thinking, problem solving, and analytical, inductive, and deductive thinking. Its decisions and choices typically involve a pause as it takes data in, draws conclusions, and then acts on this information.

The limbic brain, on the other hand, responds instantaneously with primal emotional and physical reactions to the world that revolve around fear, safety, pain, pleasure, hurt, and anger. Our limbic brain is the sensitive and reactive part of us. And our two brains may find themselves in disagreement, in which the logical brain is telling us we are safe, while the limbic brain has an entirely different opinion. Can you guess which brain usually wins? If you guessed the limbic brain, then you are absolutely right! We don't have to look too far for an example of the two brains being in conflict. Have you ever told yourself you weren't going to eat a certain food, like dessert, bread, or candy, when you were out to eat? What happened? Did you notice that one part of the brain was saying no while another part of you was saying yes, yes, yes to eating the food? Who won? Was it your good intentions or your lusty limbic brain?

This is exactly the type of disconnect that went on with Kate. During her days of overeating, her cerebral brain and limbic brain were communicating and expressing themselves in two entirely different tongues, with neither of them understanding or in agreement with the other. Her cerebral brain was screaming that it had had enough of being overweight, and it was searching for a logical and cognitive solution (i.e., another diet), while her limbic brain was tenaciously erupting like a volcano, with no interest in a rational containment, and screaming for food.

Safety and Change Go Hand in Hand

If the idea that we can pin our disorders and dysfunctions on our survival instinct still sounds a bit abstract and obtuse to you, let's take a few more examples. Consider Janet, whose life, like Kate's, became dominated by her survival instinct. For Janet it began like it had hundreds of times before—catching a plane, then a taxi, which drove her to where she was scheduled to speak on the topic of world hunger. Even though she always built in a buffer of several hours in case something unanticipated led to a delay, on this particular day it wasn't enough. A two-hour holdup on the tarmac followed by rush-hour traffic meant she had no chance of getting there on time.

When she finally arrived at her destination thirty minutes late for a sixty-minute talk, she was extremely ramped up. The combination of her lateness and built-in, ordinary anxiety prior to giving a talk made for the perfect cocktail of sheer panic. Her heart pounded as her head began to sweat, her hands tingled, and she found herself blushing in a mental fog. She had difficulty concentrating as the panic attack descended on her. Luckily, Janet managed to fumble her way through her speech, and she was relieved when it was all done. At the time, she chalked it up to "one of those things." But when she appeared for her next talk a few weeks later—on time, no less—she experienced the same disturbing panic attack.

Searching for a solution, Janet went to see her doctor, who prescribed Klonopin, an antianxiety medication that she was instructed to take before her next talk, which would inhibit a panic reaction. This seemed to solve the problem for at least her next six or seven presentations, but she needed more and more of the medication to preserve her composure. She noticed that more medication meant she felt less mentally sharp and articulate. Janet felt stuck between a rock and a hard place, and eventually began turning down speaking engagements altogether.

But it didn't stop there, for Janet was also an actress, and she began declining auditions for television shows. Her career had once flourished as she landed a number of high-profile TV gigs, but by the time she came to see me, her panic attacks were enough to keep her away from all speaking engagements and auditions. Janet felt vulnerable, as if she no longer had control over her life, and the thought of having an attack was terrifying.

So how does vulnerability relate to Janet's panic attacks? As I learned in my work with her, she had been overweight as a child and experienced a lot of teasing and rejection as a result. Now, thirty years later, the prospect of having anxiety symptoms in front of an audience represented the risk of being judged harshly and appearing stupid—which was the epitome of rejection. (As an aside, fear of rejection is also a strong emotion that's likely tied to our survival instincts; long ago we needed to be accepted within our social group just to stay alive through the help of others and to procreate.) The mere anticipation of this rejection was so horrifying and uncomfortable that Janet was willing to do anything to avoid it. Even though it wasn't logical, it really didn't matter, and Janet couldn't talk herself out of it. This was a sure case of the survival instinct seizing control of her life to keep her from experiencing discomfort and harm.

This instinct is so pervasive today that it can dominate and, quite frankly, erode our personal and work relationships. Another example is Allison, who'd had a slew of disappointing and unsuccessful relationships with men, the last one of which left her physically sick from the heartache. The mere anticipation of another relationship would trigger fear and pain in her limbic brain, as well as nausea and headaches, courtesy of her survival instinct. As this instinct took action to alleviate the discomfort (the fear of rejection), it strove to create safety in any way it could. In Allison's case, this meant refusing to accept future dates or to put herself in a situation in which she could meet a man.

Although Janet and Allison would have liked nothing more than to feel a greater sense of ease and comfort, their compelling need to alleviate their discomfort became the driving force in their lives, and a formidable obstacle to creating change. The need to banish their discomfort and generate instant safety ultimately took precedence over the need for self-improvement. Hence, change is possible only if it's truly *safe* to change.

Let me bring in one final example, which I think many people can relate to: the chronic insomniac. To think that an insomniac may actually be avoiding sleep to allay fears or feelings of discomfort seems illogical and counterintuitive, but not when you consider that the ability to fall asleep depends on our inherent need to feel safe and in control. But what happens when sleep inadvertently becomes associated with losing control? Although the insomnia could have started harmlessly one night following a bad day at work, after a series of sleepless nights, a fear of letting go begins to reign supreme over the biological need to sleep. In fact, one of the ways in which our survival instinct deals with fear is by getting in the way of us letting go, or by holding us back. This explains why many people who've suffered a heart attack develop terrible insomnia: They equate letting go and falling asleep with dying. It's true that surrendering to the sleepy feeling is as close as we can get to surrendering to death. And because this is frightening, the survival instinct restrains the sleepy feeling and interferes with it.

Obvious questions that you might be pondering at this point: Why can't these people see the train wreck coming? How can a single bad experience erupt into a chronic problem? Why can't our instincts help us out long before we're essentially paralyzed and require serious help? Sometimes, we can and do notice the red flags in the distance, but we may minimize their gravity or ignore them entirely, just as James did. Because we're genetically wired for survival, we can adapt to change with little conscious consideration. This inherent capacity to acclimate to new environments, including those that could be hostile or unhealthy, inadvertently allows us to put our head in the sand, until circumstances lead to a crisis that forces us to pay attention and take action.

Also, rather than asking ourselves why we can't sleep soundly or manage our stomach pain at night, let's face it—it's far easier to take a sleep aid or painkiller. In lieu of figuring out what's at the core of our symptoms, we reach for relief at the drugstore and force our bodies to adjust to this new environment of chronic insomnia or intestinal distress. We begin to accept and tolerate a suboptimal way of living, oblivious to opportunities to change before our health takes a bigger turn for the worse. But this human quality should not be judged harshly, for it's our nature to acclimate and not take action until a real crisis emerges. No doubt this attribute has helped us survive as a species, but for this next century, our survival may in fact depend on a whole other paradigm: **being able to weather the storm of discomfort in healthy ways, and becoming much more tolerant of discomfort, like warriors, turning sources of discomfort into sources of power.**

But before we get to the how-tos of becoming a warrior, which is the crux of part 2, we have to answer many important questions in preparation, starting with the following: What is the true nature of discomfort? What characterizes discomfort from a practical perspective, and what are the outward signs that your discomfort is reaching critical levels, potentially putting you at risk for health issues and other challenges in life? These are the questions we're going to address next, and you'll get a chance to take a quiz to determine where you fall on the spectrum of discomfort.

Chapter 3

The Balancing Act

The Delicate Sway Between Calm and Catastrophe

What if you could live with feelings of great discomfort most of the time—without those feelings having a negative effect on your behavior and health? What if you could harness a certain power in times of uncertainty and still find a measure of inner peace and happiness no matter what? What if you could turn fear into safety and discover a more enduring well-being despite the challenges and adversity you face?

You can, when you learn how to tame a part of you that lives in an old room in your brain, commanding so much of your behavior and health every minute of every day, from how you work and relate to others to how you raise your kids, express love, make decisions, and plan for the future.

In the opening chapters, I introduced you to the concept of being uncomfortable—how our lives are increasingly dominated by our growing aversion to discomfort, which has fueled an increase in chronic conditions and unhealthy habits as well as a persistent reliance on medications or harmful behavioral changes. Now I'm going to take you on a journey of what's really behind those uncomfortable feelings. Then we'll take a much closer look at the various command centers of our brains, which often don't agree with one another.

Too Close for Comfort

I have a confession to make. The book I began writing thousands of hours ago actually had an entirely different emphasis. It focused primarily on the various kinds of unhealthy habits that can materialize in our lives. But it wasn't until I found myself going through the most miserable and heartbreaking time in my life that the real focus of this book was born. After twenty-eight years of marriage, I found myself heading toward a divorce. Within the course of a few short months, my life unraveled as I went through a wrenching and devastating transition. This wasn't the first time that I had endured a tremendous loss, for my mother's passing some years ago had left me equally devastated. But the loss of my marriage and immediate family as I knew it was crushing on an entirely different level. It was an experience so raw and agonizing as to be surreal and unbelievable to a part of me that couldn't accept what I was going through. Somewhere, deep down, I told myself that a silver lining had to exist, but in those initial months of absolute misery, I could see nothing but the opposite of good. I felt tortured by sadness, grief, and my sense of responsibility. I so desperately wanted relief that medications were tempting, seeming like such an easy solution, especially when my physician offered them to me. I kept asking myself, "Is the piercing pain related to the need to feel punished, keeping me from moving forward with my life? Or does it serve a more useful purpose by offering me insights and strengthening me, helping me grow in ways I am not fully aware of yet?"

As you can imagine, the psychologist in me started examining the pain and discomfort separately from the divorce. I began to try to understand my relationship with these feelings, especially when I felt my heart pound or my mind race, and when I cried and sensed my body scream with genuine physical pain. I noticed how, instinctively, I ached to vanquish the pain and not have to contend with it—to seek ways to quickly turn it off. Of course this naturally made drugs such as those to enhance my sleep, control my anxiety, or level my mood all the more attractive. I also could see how food or drinking could become a great diversion or escape hatch. And thanks to my experience in psychology, I was able to acutely observe the fact that this undeniable desire for fast relief wasn't a cognitive process, but was rather a gut response—an instinctual reaction rooted in primal fear. In other words, as I focused on my pain, I noticed how it aroused a certain fear in me, fear that I somehow wouldn't be able to tolerate my discomfort and that something "bad" would soon happen, that I would die or another terrible event would mar my life.

This self-examination continued. I could see how I was wired to avoid pain as a human. Long ago we evolved to take action when we felt pain, which no doubt has its adaptive properties, allowing us to survive. We've been wired to dodge the kind of pain and discomfort that could really kill us. But today, we're rarely faced with life-threatening situations. I wondered about the potential downside of our body's natural reactions, especially to petty nuisances that aren't so lethal. In other words, I started to wonder if my old, obsolete wiring was potentially getting in the way of experiencing more personal growth.

This was when I had my aha moment. **I began to understand that to truly grow (and to move forward in my life, beyond the divorce), I needed to change my relationship with pain and discomfort. If I didn't, then I would be pursuing my life in a defensive and guarded manner. My prewired instincts would, in effect, continue to run my life.**

Forming a brand-new relationship with pain has taken some time, but no sooner did I start to simply change my perspective did I learn that I could tolerate much more discomfort than I ever thought possible. This doesn't mean it was easy, because truth be told, it can still be a struggle. But the end result is that I've become more comfortable with being uncomfortable, and I now know from experience that I can survive it. Today I view emotional and physical health in a whole new light. **It's not defined as being a state in which there's an absence of pain, but rather a state in which one can find comfort and safety *in the face of discomfort.*** To achieve this, I had to retrain my instinctual wiring to no longer press the panic button whenever it anticipated or experienced discomfort. I can't say that I enjoy this ongoing process, but I've come to accept it as a part of life. **Put another way, true health and happiness, I have learned, is not about merely having a life full of comfort and pleasure. Much to the contrary, it's about the ability to feel safe and comfortable despite life's inevitable hardships, drawbacks, and challenges.**

As I came to understand all of this, I began reevaluating the work I had done with my patients over the years, realizing that I had actually been doing so much more than altering their inner safety. In addition, I had been helping them deal with their own fears related to pain and discomfort all along.

And it became evident to me that a universal experience among my patients was a profound undercurrent of discomfort, which sustained many of their health challenges. Their perceived fear of losing control over their rising level of discomfort ultimately provided a fertile ground for behaviors to develop that compromised their health. So whether I was treating a patient who could not sleep at night or one who suffered from chronic pain and panic attacks, they both shared the inability to tolerate discomfort and shift out of unhealthy habits.

When I hear patients lament that they are afraid of hunger, afraid of insomnia, afraid to ride in elevators or airplanes, afraid to speak in public, or afraid to have intimate relationships, they often all have the same underlying antagonist: an overly sensitive survival instinct. Which means they have the same solution: taming their survival instinct while making their fear- and pain-based discomfort more tolerable and comfortable. **Indeed, if you can overcome your gut response to feeling uncomfortable, you can heal yourself.**

Misalignment: The Heart of Being Uncomfortable

From a cultural standpoint, discomfort has had a long history in the story of humankind, especially as it relates to suffering. One can argue that entire religions are grounded in communities' needs to assuage suffering. In some traditions, suffering, or the absence of pleasure and certain comforts in life, is seen as a pathway to purification, that somehow it can bring you closer to God or the eternal being, and away from the distraction and lure of hedonistic pleasures. And let's not forget what our own parents taught many of us early on: that suffering and hardship is a necessary fact of life, and that it's part of what allows us to succeed. After all, "no pain, no gain." In a similar vein, we were taught to believe that what doesn't kill us makes us stronger. But let's turn to the more fundamental, practical definition of *discomfort.*

If I were to ask you what it means to experience discomfort, your definition might include words such as *angst, pain, restlessness, uneasiness, edginess,* and *misery.* Feeling discomfort may very well be inherently part of the human condition. And it's no stranger to us, for we typically do what we can to avoid it or get rid of it as soon as possible. Discomfort is not just an annoyance or a simple preoccupation; it's typically something that can be quite frightening and overwhelming, particularly if we cannot resolve it. We learn early on what it is, whether it's falling and scraping our knee as a child, or feeling the dread of talking in front of a large group, our heart rocketing out of our chest.

Animals experience discomfort, too, but with humans it's different because of our higher brain function. We can be much more aware of it and attribute a broader spectrum of triggers to various levels of discomfort. So not only do physical realities such as a sprained ankle or a laceration trigger discomfort, but so also do more subtle situations in which we find ourselves feeling terribly on edge but cannot identify the root cause.

There are actually two types of discomfort. One is acute, such as a broken arm or a skinned knee. But more often, discomfort falls within the second category, the one in which it's chronic and much more insidious in nature. This type of discomfort lingers over long periods of time and is not merely physical, but psychological as well.

It's unquestionable that discomfort has served a constructive purpose throughout much of our evolutionary history, starting when we were roaming the savannas. Back then, we'd have to rely on our sensations of discomfort to tell us what situations or foods to avoid that would precipitate pain, illness, or death. If we'd been harmed by another, discomfort told us whom to avoid or when to take up arms in order to avert future harm or other serious hazards. But in today's world, these primitive needs for protection seldom arise, and most often we suffer discomfort at our own hands. **Indeed, the majority of discomfort is typically self-manufactured.** In other words, we are often the perpetrator of our own inner discomfort. As Mark Twain once wrote, "My life has been filled with terrible misfortunes—most of which never happened." We are our own worst enemy.

So with the lack of an external battle or enemy, an internal battle has emerged. What's more, our discomfort today typically revolves around trivial issues that are construed by our mind and body as being ruinous. The war that then takes place within us isn't just confined to our minds—it also materializes at the cellular level. Nowhere else is this so obvious as in autoimmune illnesses, which are characterized by the absence of an external threat yet the body begins to wage a war within itself, one that takes a serious and sometimes deadly toll.

Regardless of which kind of chronic discomfort we're talking about, they all share one common feature: mismanagement or misalignment. Lingering discomfort indicates that we are not drawing on our inner resources and not paying attention and learning what our body is trying to tell us. In other words, chronic discomfort is a function of how much misalignment exists within us and between us and the outside world. Now, that may seem like an incredibly esoteric concept, but let me explain. It's much simpler than it seems.

It's easy at first to overlook the early stages of discomfort, the signs of which can be any number of things—nagging fatigue, forgetfulness, foggy concentration, achy joints, a spate of headaches, an upset stomach, feeling unrested after a full night's sleep, irritability, or low patience. After experiencing any one of these signals, we can ignore them, essentially disregarding them as if they are simply the status quo. Or if we do acknowledge them, we may reach for different medications to manage the symptoms, rather than turning to our inner ability to restore balance. Contrary to what many people think, the human body is remarkably capable of healing itself thanks to built-in physiological "technology" that's already programmed within our cells. To understand this, look no further than our antibodies, which are made to automatically launch when they detect an incoming invader or pathogen. But rather than rely on this innate technology, we are quick to turn to external forms of relief.

One of the most prominent examples of this is seen in the increasing number of children and adults being diagnosed with attention deficit hyperactivity disorder (ADHD). And for sure, ADHD most definitely is at work among a certain small portion of the population. But scores more people are getting this diagnosis every day since the parameters for defining ADHD have been widely expanded.

Although the increase in the number of ADHD patients could be blamed on the fact that people are more aware of this condition and thus it's more readily diagnosed, we cannot neglect another driving force: the drug companies behind much of the research, who'd like nothing better than to find proof that there's a greater need and demand for drugs to treat ADHD. This isn't too dissimilar to what's happened in the realm of cholesterol studies: By continuing to broaden the definition of what's considered problematic, pharmaceutical companies can sell more cholesterol-reducing drugs.

But what is so commonly overlooked is that many people diagnosed with ADHD could tame a large portion of their symptoms just by being able to better manage their levels of discomfort. Certainly, part of the problem is cultural, as demands at work and home increase and become overwhelming. But part of the problem is also a factor of skills training. Rarely do we learn how to manage discomfort that accompanies escalating demands. So we come to feel defenseless, and turn to external solutions as a reflex.

A State of Agitance

Contrary to what you might think, chronic discomfort is not something that comes on suddenly or out of the blue. It's the consequence of a subtle but powerful subversive undercurrent that I call "agitance," which is what tends to build up silently before we even sense discomfort.

As with the initial signs of discomfort, it's easy to turn a blind eye to agitance as it quietly brews. A great way to understand this concept is to think of agitance as working like our core or basal body temperature. Normal is considered 98.6 degrees Fahrenheit. But this can be influenced by other factors, such as exercise that ticks it upward a notch, or illness that triggers a fever. But acute stress and emotion can also influence your temperature. Small fluctuations are often unnoticeable (in fact, the medical community doesn't acknowledge a change in temperature as significant until the temperature reaches 100 degrees). But those who are tuned in to a shift from 98.6 to 100 degrees may notice a warmth in their body; a slight fogginess, edginess, or restlessness; or the need for more time to fall asleep. So from a metaphorical standpoint, the higher the level of agitance, the higher the "temperature," and the more noticeable these types of symptoms become. But when the temperature crosses 100 degrees, or the agitance level begins to spike above this level, a sense of discomfort emerges. Once this happens, you notice the change in substantial and undeniable signs—significant brain fog, fatigue, aches, difficulty concentrating, high irritability, and a short temper. These symptoms indicate your agitance level has crossed the line into the discomfort zone.

Now, even though you notice discomfort at this point, as I've discussed, you can still find ways to minimize it. For example, using the analogy of rising body temperature, it's easy to pop an aspirin or ibuprofen to lower your temperature and manage symptoms. Yet if these discomfort signals continue to be ignored or artificially quelled, that core body temperature may, metaphorically speaking, hit dangerously high levels—upwards of 103. At this unfortunate point, the brain and body take action to preserve the safety of the organism before serious organ damage occurs.

To help further your understanding of agitance and bring this home for you, let's ask a question: How agitated are you right this moment? Answering this question using the following checklist will help you to really grasp what agitance means, how it distinguishes itself from traditional stress, and what kind of role it plays in your life. Virtually everyone is familiar with what it feels like to be off kilter, out of balance, worked up, or unsettled. But how much do you bear every day? Find out. To test your current level of agitance, use my Agitance Checklist.

The Agitance Checklist

The following checklist will help you to gauge your level of agitance by measuring those activities or behaviors that typically stoke it. Answer each question honestly and to the best of your ability. No one has to see your responses; they are your own. Knowing the answers to these questions will help you to maximize the content and exercises in this book. You might find it helpful to go beyond the simple yes/no response and take note of any additional details that come to mind.

1. Are you constantly checking your e-mails?
2. When you are suddenly or unexpectedly faced with free time, do you fairly quickly reach for your phone to check for messages, go online, or call someone?
3. Are you checking for e-mails and texts even when there is no indication you received one?
4. If you do not receive an e-mail or text after a certain period of time, do you feel anxious, uneasy, or even depressed?

5. If you send a text or e-mail, do you become uneasy if you do not receive an immediate reply?
6. If you are in line at a grocery store or post office and the clerk is new or taking his or her time, are you easily agitated?
7. When it is nearing bedtime, do you look for reasons to stay up, and therefore resist getting into bed?
8. At nighttime or on weekends, when you are not at work, are you uncomfortable when you are not busy or even working?
9. Do you like the feeling of being wired?
10. Do you find it difficult to slow down?
11. Do you get bored easily and as a result constantly seek stimulation?
12. When you feel uneasy, do you reach for food to calm you?
13. Are you uncomfortable in idle time without structure?
14. Do you drive fast even when you are not in a rush or are not late for an appointment?
15. Do you walk quickly even when you are not in a rush?
16. Are you impatient with others even when you aren't in a rush?
17. Do you take things too personally (and get all riled up) when you shouldn't?
18. When you are bored, do you find yourself searching for food even if you aren't hungry?
19. When you are hungry, do you feel unsettled if you cannot eat in a timely manner?
20. When you think about food, do you find yourself wanting to eat, even though you aren't hungry?
21. Do you stay angry longer than necessary—when it no longer serves a purpose?

22. When you seek stimulation, does it need to be multisensory, such as eating while reading or watching TV?
23. Do you find it difficult to turn your mind off at bedtime?
24. If you awaken in the middle of the night, does your mind become so active that you cannot return to sleep quickly and easily?
25. Are you fearful or uncomfortable deviating from the familiar and expected?
26. Do you find yourself obsessing about things of little value or importance, or things that have no connection to reality?
27. Do you find yourself feeling pressured to get everything done and feeling agitated when you can't?
28. If something isn't exactly as you wanted and expected, do you become agitated?
29. Do you expect perfection from yourself?
30. Do you expect perfection from *others*?
31. When you are on vacation, or supposed to be relaxing, do you find yourself still worked up, and looking to be constantly busy?
32. Are you uncomfortable with uncertainty?

Scoring: If you answered yes to just one question, then you likely have some degree of agitance working inside you, although it's probably manageable and you may barely recognize it. If you answered yes to five to nine questions, then your agitance level is likely noticeable but still relatively manageable. If you answered yes to ten or more questions, then you're entering a zone in which your agitance is increasingly more palpable, and is probably leading (or will soon lead) to physical or mental symptoms of discomfort.

Agitance is a normal, inevitable part of life. There will always be competing forces working in our lives, both inside our bodies and out. In many cases, agitance remains below the radar and isn't bothersome. It's happening all the time, right down to the cellular level. Without us realizing it, for instance, our body is constantly working to keep our blood sugars balanced while attending to competing needs among the various organs and systems. Different areas of our brains are perpetually jockeying for position. Our blood pressure can be balanced, while our cholesterol levels are not, or vice versa. In scientific circles, doctors call the body's need for balance "homeostasis," which is constancy in the face of environmental fluctuations. The whole point of regulation is to maintain the body in a relatively constant state. Yes, it's dynamic and changing all the time, but the body continually modifies itself to create the steadiness that it craves—to stay in a zone where it's safe and protected from harm. If you think about it, the body is perpetually under forces that work against constancy, such as your choosing when to eat and what time you'll surrender to sleep and go to bed. Even the temperature of your environment keeps your body working to maintain a steady 98.6 degrees.

What we often don't think about, however, is that such a balancing act takes place on a larger scale as well. We are constantly striving for a complete or comprehensive state of alignment outside us, too, across all areas of our lives. When we achieve a full state of alignment, I call this "resonance." Unfortunately, resonance is rare, and when it does occur, it's fleeting. More typically, we can achieve balance or alignment in one area of our life, but not in another. For example, you may find that your work life is well balanced, while your personal relationships are not, or vice versa. Or maybe you enjoy your work, but are dogged by physical illness. Of course, there are plenty of situations in which we find congruency, or compatibility, with others, or with a profession that's aligned with our strengths and attributes. Additionally, we can experience situational alignment, such as when we feel one with our environment on a beautiful hike through the woods. Others might feel this within the buzz of the city in which they grew up. We can also experience this alignment with loved ones, that feeling of being simpatico with another individual, such as a soul mate or someone we've known for years with whom there is a strong bond and no tension. We can experience this among a group of close friends, feeling at home when we are hanging out with these special people. But unfortunately, since we live in a world that is constantly changing, we are destined to find ourselves being yanked away from the things we love and that represent alignment to us. And, as we all know, these types of situations are often just a small part of our lives, making some level of misalignment inescapable. The ephemeral nature of life's experiences makes permanent resonance impossible. Circumstances change; people change; life is as much a moving target as is our quest to achieve alignment and resonance. It can become harder and harder to find true alignment even across several areas of our lives today in all that we do, which is why many people feel at a loss.

Put another way, we can feel as if we're living in a chronic state of misalignment, never balanced, always on edge. If we're in real physical pain that distracts us from addressing other primary needs such as love or pleasure, our misalignment continues to deepen. Or, we can become too reliant on external sources of pleasure at the expense of internal well-being and peace. In all these cases, there is a spiraling level of agitance, a growing lack of harmony, or misalignment, and an escalating unease—ultimately a recipe for increasing levels of discomfort, which then triggers fear and eventually an overly activated survival instinct.

Let me be clear: Agitance itself does not represent a problem, for it's an inevitable by-product of living in our world. It poses a problem, however, when there are a number of factors or situations tripping it, when there is little opportunity for it to reset and lower, and when it begins to result in significant misalignments in our world. For example, we may find ourselves wanting to stay up late to work on the computer, return e-mails, watch shows that we've recorded, or catch up on newspapers and magazines that are piled up on our desk and in our bedroom. But the desire to do this may conflict with an increasing inner fatigue and the body's physiological need to sleep. In other words, *the more agitance we feel, the more out of sync we become with our inner and outside worlds. And the more out of sync we become, the greater the level of misalignment.*

One of the more striking examples of this is when there's an unnecessary need for constant stimulation. You may have experienced this yourself when, after a hectic, crisis-filled day or week, you resist slowing down and instead look for ways to remain keyed up, such as by staying up late to watch the news or surf the Internet, seeking tasks to complete, and wolfing down sugary foods. Over time we can become addicted to this type of overstimulation and turn into agitance junkies. By then, we've reached the point where our agitance has gone beyond our physical and psychological abilities to adapt to or accommodate it.

It should come as no surprise that the greater the alignment, the less the agitance.

With an understanding of what agitance is and how it manifests in our behaviors, the next obvious question is, how do we manage our escalating agitance levels? Like controlling discomfort, this is something we are seldom taught, but it can dramatically affect our lives.

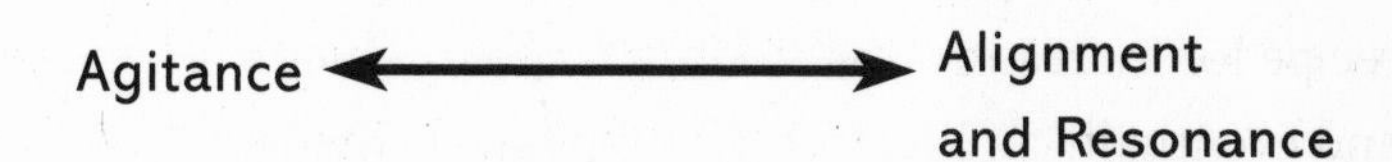

Agitance can be managed effectively or ineffectively. When it's being managed well, this is known as alignment. This is where we want to be. At the other end of the spectrum is a full-blown state of agitance. If we experience alignment across multiple parts of our lives, then this is resonance.

A State of Stress

It's important to distinguish the difference between stress and agitance, as well as between stress and discomfort. *Agitance* and *stress* are not synonymous, and neither are *discomfort* and *stress*. For the purposes of this book, stress relates to a distinct event or situation, such as dealing with a demanding or surly boss, a deadline, an important exam, or a job interview. In these situations, our aggravation and anxiety can be clearly pinpointed to specific circumstances; the cause of the stress is something precise and focused. In contrast, agitance levels are caused not necessarily by one particular event or setting, but by a buildup of imbalances. They can be ongoing and independent of certain circumstances, accumulating and gathering steam over time. Stress levels can rise and fall with respect to a specific event.

That said, there is a very important relationship between agitance and stress. As agitance levels are managed poorly and we become more revved up, we are far more vulnerable to the effects of stress. Recall Janet from the previous chapter whose travel delays led to a complete state of panic. Certainly, those delays added a layer of unanticipated stress to her already elevated agitance levels. Separately, neither her stress nor her agitance would have led to her panic reaction. But the confluence of the two catapulted her into the discomfort zone of the survival instinct.

Conversely, if we learn to manage our agitance levels better, our reaction to stressful events can be controlled, taking a much lower toll on us. It may also help to think of agitance as an inner speed that is affected by stressful events. A low level of agitance might be twenty miles per hour. Consider, for instance, that your agitance levels may be traveling at a speed of 40 mph within the body, but once you add a stressful event, your speed is elevated to 70 mph—crossing the 60 mph threshold, at which point the mind and body become acutely aware of feelings of discomfort. And when this discomfort level continues to rise, such as to 90 mph, it is experienced as an absolute threat to our survival—even when the threat is imagined or trivial.

From a practical standpoint, you might not notice the difference between stress and agitance, even though you can attribute your stress to particular events or circumstances in your life. The overall feeling is the same: flustered, on edge, unstrung, unnerved, tense, tired, or any combination of these. But it's important to realize that all of us carry around a baseline level of agitance and that these two factors interact in ways that elevate our sense of discomfort in the world. The more we find ourselves shouldering the weight of stress, which adds to that baseline level of agitance, the more likely we are to feel uncomfortable. And the more uncomfortable we get, the closer we come to awakening that survival instinct. Over time, as our survival instinct is increasingly triggered, our tolerance for discomfort shrinks. In other words, less and less discomfort is needed to precipitate the survival instinct. And as our instinctual reactions to discomfort increase, our fears only continue to worsen and deepen, opening the door much wider for behaviors to set in that attempt to help us escape the discomfort.

Discomfort levels and how they are experienced can strongly vary between people. We all know people who weather the storms in their life better than others. Some can successfully manage higher levels of discomfort—living at much higher speeds—while others are able to tolerate only low levels and have discomfort thresholds at lower speeds. This can change, however, in both directions:

Someone who fights discomfort all the time can become less and less capable of dealing with it, and someone who learns to handle discomfort in healthy ways can increase their wiggle room for it.

This is an important point, because many believe that experiencing high levels of discomfort ultimately leads to a stronger individual. Some people recite the statement "If it doesn't kill me, then it will make me stronger." The actual data on this indicates otherwise. Over time, chronic adversity does in fact weaken people rather than make them stronger. Gaining from perpetual pain or adversity is true only if the individual is capable of managing these higher levels of discomfort. But if and when they become unmanageable, it's like the whole mind and body become overly sensitive to smaller levels of discomfort. And as we experience a greater sensitivity to discomfort, it takes less and less discomfort to unleash the survival instinct.

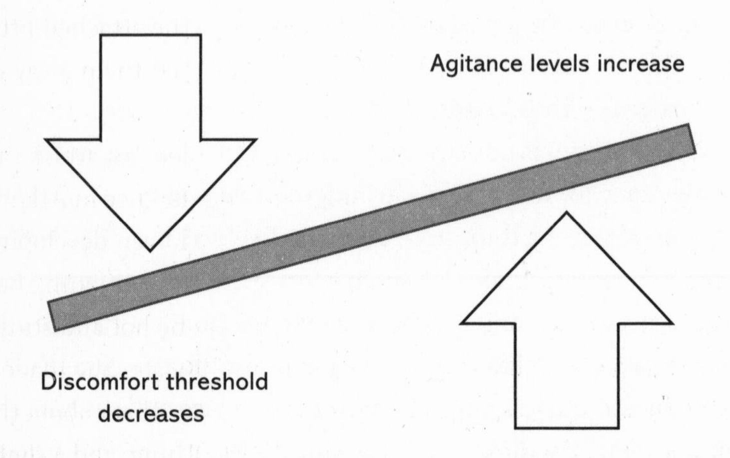

Let's take another example that will help sum up all these points.

Andrea was a senior executive at a major Hollywood studio. She had significant responsibilities and work demands. So it wasn't unusual for her to work in the evenings and on weekends. Yet even after her work was completed, she found herself still involved with the computer and answering e-mails that were nonessential—factors that are highly related to elevated agitance levels. This resulted in not only a delayed bedtime but also a poor diet, for she had little time to focus on healthy eating. But unlike someone who hated her job and resented the obligations, Andrea actually enjoyed her work immensely, and said she was "lucky to have it," so the expectations placed on her weren't experienced as stressful. Over time, however, her growing agitance levels began to stoke a greater misalignment between her physical and psychological needs. For the most part she didn't notice her rising agitance, even when she felt tired and unrefreshed in the mornings. But eventually this lifestyle would take a toll. At some point she began to feel a number of small aches and pains when she awakened. These were the first signs of her agitance levels beginning to cross her threshold and lead to noticeable discomfort. Initially, she attached little importance to her symptoms and easily explained them away as just a fact of getting older.

It wasn't until Andrea suffered what she called "an attack out of nowhere" while attending a summer work conference in Atlanta that she was forced to pay attention to what had been developing beneath the radar of her consciousness. The air-conditioning had malfunctioned, causing the conference room to be hot and stuffy, and she suddenly felt as if she was going to suffocate. She made a hasty exit and ran to splash cool water on her face. That's about the time she noticed a rapid heartbeat, shallow breathing, and a slight dizziness. She was also experiencing anger and sadness, evidenced by her tears. All these were clear indicators that her survival instinct had been triggered.

Once this incident was over, she assumed that it had been just a random event and would likely never reappear. But then it happened again, and again—whenever she attended meetings, particularly if the room felt mildly stuffy or had poor air circulation. She'd begin to sweat and feel anxious. In other words, now only mild or moderate discomfort was capable of precipitating her survival instinct and similar "attacks." Andrea had been in a lot of hot conference rooms before and had never had this reaction, so it seemed odd to her that she would react to it now. For most people, being in a hot and stuffy room will elicit some edginess. And for most people, just like for Andrea so many times in the past, this experience doesn't trigger a fear response. But for Andrea that summer day in Atlanta, the circumstances were in place for her to have a full-blown attack. It was the unexpected collision of elevated agitance levels and misalignments in Andrea's life with the hot and stuffy room that pushed her into the discomfort zone of the survival instinct.

What makes this case example meaningful and so emblematic of others' experiences is that Andrea had been subject to chronic high agitance and increasing discomfort for some time. She had managed to live with it for the most part and overlook it, but when this discomfort ticked upward and extended beyond her threshold due to the circumstance of that stuffy room, it precipitated her survival instinct's fear reaction. From that point on, it took very little discomfort to trigger a fearful response. Now just low levels of discomfort or the mere anticipation of being uncomfortable became enough to provoke a full-fledged survival instinct response.

Andrea might never have had this reaction if she had learned to recognize and respect her growing agitance and budding discomfort. If these had been better managed, sitting in a sweltering room would have probably just felt like a nuisance and nothing more. My work with Andrea ultimately entailed building up her tolerance for discomfort and helping her learn how to healthily manage her agitance by training her survival instinct to distinguish between true threats to her survival and trivial annoyances.

It is a common misconception that if we are unaware of agitance levels, then they must be innocuous. Much to the contrary, our agitance can have a tremendous physical effect that goes unnoticed because we don't experience any symptoms right away. But deep within we could already be experiencing physical repercussions, such as high blood pressure or increased blood sugar levels—all of which can go undetected for some time. The fact is, as I described with Andrea, the ultimate outcome of high agitance levels is a collision with the survival instinct.

The Past Predicts the Present and Future

It's all relative! By that I mean that our present experience with discomfort is often a function of past experiences. For example, if we've felt fear and anxiety in uncomfortable situations before, as well as an inability to perform well or focus, then this predisposes us to feel like this under similar circumstances. Another way of appreciating this phenomenon is to simply consider what happens when you hear an old song that brings up a rich assortment of memories. It's the same with discomfort. So our experience of discomfort in the present can become overly magnified by our past history, making us much more vulnerable to greater fear or lack of safety.

Something else I want to point out is that there's also a tendency to experience and understand discomfort from an absolute perspective. That is, we are either uncomfortable or not. But people may function for long periods of time with a certain level of discomfort, and then something clicks, and suddenly they find that they can no longer tolerate it. So discomfort is less absolute than we think. It's an experience that waxes and wanes. The goal is to know how to tolerate it whether it's at a maximum or a minimum.

So how does discomfort fit into our challenges with the survival instinct? What causes our survival instinct to become so overworked and overly sensitive today? I've hinted at some of the causes already, most of which relate to our brains' being ill equipped to deal with modern culture. Now, however, we're going to delve into the nitty-gritty details of this problem's root cause, starting with a look at the physiology of our limbic system and how it predisposes us to an overreactive survival instinct. It will provide the foundation you need to then take control of your instincts for good.

Chapter 4
The Seat of the Survival Instinct
The Biology of Fear

In the previous chapter we discussed the role of agitance and discomfort as they relate to the survival instinct. Now, we're going to turn our attention to where these reactions take place in the brain and body. As we have discussed, the mind and body are constantly seeking balance. But so often this balance, or alignment, is fleeting, and unfortunately undermined by chronic states of agitance. Although agitance can represent an incongruity between us and the outside world, more frequently it originates chiefly from a lack of balance *within* us—between our cells and in our biochemistry, nervous system, and even brain. In fact, it's within the brain that most of the jockeying takes place. Once agitance levels are no longer manageable, we begin to feel discomfort both physically and emotionally. The question is, What, exactly, is going on in this subtle yet profound cascade of events? How is this all possible? That's what we're going to explore.

One Head, Three Brains

We humans are actually the proud owners of three separate brains, all reflecting different stages of development and evolution. Our first and oldest brain dates back to the time of reptiles. We continue to share this part of the brain with reptiles and birds. For us, it's housed in the brain stem and cerebellum. Not surprisingly, this ancient part of us governs very basic but vital functions, and receives direct input from our entire body. For example, the brain stem is involved in the regulation of our heartbeat, breathing, blood pressure, circulation, digestion, and the famous fight-or-flight response. The brain stem includes the medulla, pons, tectum, reticular formation, and tegmentum. The cerebellum is involved in the orchestration of our body's movement. This region of the brain is sometimes called the R-complex, with the *R* representing *reptile*. What stands out about this part of the brain is that it's emotionless, and is strictly instinctual and automatic. It's what saves us without our needing to think or feel much of anything.

It wasn't until we evolved into mammals that the next level of brain development occurred. This part would become the limbic brain, which sits on top of the brain stem and cerebellum. The limbic brain receives input from the brain stem, attaching emotions to these impulses. This is why mammals, such as humans, primates, dogs, cats, and dolphins, all have emotional responses to their world. But like the brain stem, the limbic brain's responses are often outside of awareness and are automatic.

In the next stage of evolution, mammals developed a new part of the brain, layered on top of the limbic brain, called the cerebral cortex. The more evolved the mammal is, the larger the cerebral cortex. And the larger the cortex, the more developed the brain function is. When you picture a human brain, for instance, you likely see lots of folds and creases on the outside. That's the cerebral cortex, and it follows that the more folds that exist in the cerebral cortex, the greater the surface area, which translates to more advanced capabilities. It is this part of the brain that gives us the higher reasoning abilities—the ability to think analytically and logically, problem-solve, plan for the future, and think abstractly.

As you can see, the evolution of the human brain, like civilization, went from primitive to more advanced, and each new and better "layer" was simply built above the other. By virtue of this evolution, the human species was given new tools that enhanced its survival. In other words, each new layer of sophistication equipped us with a better, more agile brain that could help us live longer and better preserve our species. With the development of the cerebral cortex, we suddenly found ourselves with much better control over our limbic impulses, or our emotional reactions to the world. This is what's called top-down brain functioning, whereby the cerebral brain regulates and attempts to control the older brains below. But it's here where the inherent problem develops, as both structures, the cerebral brain and the limbic brain, are often innately driven to assert control over one another, each presuming that its priorities are greater than the other's. The cerebral brain claims to be smarter than the limbic brain and is often quick to dismiss it, resorting to an overregulation of the limbic brain by lecturing it with logic and reasoning. But the limbic brain *feels* its needs are more pressing, and it will have nothing to do with being lectured to, so it will assert its needs in a physical manner or in an emotional manner with temper tantrums. This sets up an ongoing struggle to somehow find a balance between these two parts of our brain. Although overall the brain itself is driven to strive for balance, suffice it to say a détente is not always easily achieved. Since sustained balance is difficult to attain, we find that the cerebral and limbic brains can wax and wane in terms of their influence. And yet, the goal ultimately is to have these two separate regions work together in some sort of coordinated, harmonious way.

As I also briefly noted earlier, the limbic brain, like our reptilian brain, is very much focused on basic survival functions, providing the home ground of our more primal emotional states, particularly anger and fear. It is important to note that these primal emotions are pure; when they originate, they are without cerebral analysis, reflection, or interpretation. Put another way, they are automatic and reflexive. Since the limbic brain receives its basic impulses from the brain stem, its reactions are swift as it quickly attaches very primal emotions to these impulses that are geared toward preservation and survival. And the limbic system has a strong connection to the autonomic nervous and endocrine systems, which we'll talk about shortly. One particular area of the limbic brain that has received a substantial amount of attention related to anger and fear is the amygdala. In studies in which scientists sever the amygdala in animals, they find that the animals lose their aggressive behavior and even their ability to react normally to fear. By the same token, when scientists stimulate this area of the brain, they achieve the opposite effect—the animals exhibit more aggressive behavior.

The limbic system's actual anatomy includes the hypothalamus, the hippocampus, the amygdala, and the nucleus accumbens, or the so-called pleasure center of the brain. So within the limbic brain we find the actual physical and emotional basis for primal experiences such as hunger, pain, sleepiness, anger, fear, and pleasure. A central part of this limbic brain is the basal ganglia, which houses two important areas related to behavior—the nucleus accumbens and the ventral striatum. What makes these areas so critical is that they are connected to a neurotransmitter called dopamine and the brain's natural opiates, called endorphins. Dopamine is a brain chemical that strongly influences behavior such as habits and addictions. The endorphins influence how these habits and addictions are experienced, particularly the pleasurable aspects.

When we experience something pleasurable, these brain chemicals have a significant impact on other parts of the brain and the body to urge us to continue whatever behavior or seek whatever stimulus is creating the pleasurable sensation. Let's take an example. Many people find themselves drawn to chocolate. This has its physiological roots: Just the thought or sight of chocolate can create a dopamine surge in the limbic brain. Every time this pairing occurs—the thought or sight of chocolate and the release of dopamine—more power is established between these two things. (This can also happen in relationships, particularly during the early, infatuation phase. That rush of euphoria we feel at the mere thought or image of our new partner is made possible by a dopamine surge.) When we actually eat the chocolate, the chocolate then causes a release of opiates in the brain that stimulate our pleasure centers, which further cements our behavior of eating chocolate. What's interesting about the dopamine surge, however, is that it actually begins to drop once we get what we want and start consuming the chocolate. So it's more the mental *anticipation* of having the chocolate than the reality of eating it that creates the dopamine surge. (With relationships, we all know that those initial feelings of rapture weaken over time as those surges of dopamine fade.)

Overeaters similarly become trapped within a loop of dopamine scarcity. After a long history of bingeing on high-calorie foods, they enter a chronic state of dopamine withdrawal, which, as you can imagine, leaves them in an elevated state of discomfort. In an effort to restore their dopamine levels and feelings of comfort, they find themselves racked by compulsive cravings for the very foods that caused the problem in the first place. Of course, this pummels overeaters in two ways: Not only does the lowered dopamine make them eat more, but the actual overeating itself further reduces their dopamine levels.

On the flip side, when the limbic brain experiences fear, another process unfolds with similar outcomes. The moment we become fearful, a brain chemical called corticotrophin-releasing factor (CRF) is unleashed in different areas of the limbic region, particularly the hypothalamus and amygdala. CRF begins to drive a stress response in the body that entails a sequence of events known in scientific circles as the hypothalamic-pituitary-adrenal axis, or HPA axis, as it involves all of these components of the brain. When CRF first acts on the hypothalamus, it stimulates the release of another chemical called adrenocorticotropic hormone (ACTH) from the pituitary, which then causes the adrenal glands to release glucocorticoids, stress hormones such as cortisol. These glucocorticoids in turn increase many biological actions, affecting our blood sugar and influencing immune function. The adrenal glands respond further by launching other adrenal hormones such as epinephrine and norepinephrine, which activate the sympathetic nervous system. This is the classic fight-or-flight reaction. When it takes place, your heart rate and blood pressure increase, changing the flow of blood throughout the body. But what's most interesting about this whole process is that the CRF activation leads to *dopamine reduction*. So not only is our fear reaction physically uncomfortable and emotionally upsetting, but the reduction in dopamine creates a very negative, dysphoric feeling. And, similar to dopamine surges cementing a certain behavior, this contrary reaction does the same; the discomfort and fear reactions also cement powerful responses in the body. As a result, we feel a strong urge to somehow find a way to end this discomfort and fear in the same way the pleasurable loop drives us to maintain the pleasurable sensations through certain behaviors. This compelling desire to terminate the discomfort and imbalance is wired within us as a very basic means to assure our safety and preservation. The limbic brain's powerful wiring and undeniable need to preserve our safety at all costs is what we are calling our survival instinct.

Hence, at the heart of our rising levels of agitance and discomfort, which trigger the survival instinct, is a simple drop in our dopamine levels. Discomfort goes up, and dopamine comes down, plunging us into a vicious cycle. This explains why overeaters are driven to eat more, as I've described, or panic attack sufferers increasingly begin to avoid even innocuous situations that result in dopamine depletion. These intense reactions are based in the limbic response. Whether they are an addictive urge related to compulsive cravings for food, sex, drugs, or alcohol or are instead a compelling fear or anger response that's traveling down the HPA axis, they ultimately all represent an out-of-balance state or nonalignment within the brain. These reactions can insidiously generate other imbalances in the brain and body that further create problems rather than solving them.

Simply put, the limbic brain is vigorously driven by pleasure and pain. At one time, when we were a primitive species, this certainly had some preservation value. But as we evolved and became much more complex and sophisticated, these fundamental drives didn't evolve with us, remaining absolute rather than being attuned to subtleties. If you feel uncomfortable, for instance, then your limbic brain interprets that as a signal that your safety is being seriously threatened, which then triggers a drastic reaction to avert danger and maintain your safety. Your limbic brain by its very nature is not very effective at evaluating different degrees of discomfort and fear. Hence, being at the mercy of these primary drives severely conflicts with the needs of a more complex society and civilization, in which people cannot be constantly acting on their needs for pleasure and fear. **But this is where the survival instinct poses a problem, in**

that it doesn't easily make distinctions, and tends to view all discomfort and fear as an ultimate threat to our survival.

What's more, as people find themselves enslaved by an endless cycle of dopamine deficiency—in which certain behaviors, such as overeating and addictions, develop to ease the discomfort in the short term—the likelihood of experiencing future fear reactions is increased. And the chronic release of CRF over time decreases the amount of available dopamine. This fear circuit grows all the more sensitized such that it doesn't take much to create discomfort and provoke a survival instinct reaction. Put simply, the more discomfort we feel, the greater the likelihood we'll experience fear. And the more fearful we become, the more uncomfortable we become. These two forces feed on each other and imprison people within a dangerous spiral.

Two-Way Street, One Busier Direction

With our limbic brain having a hard time deciphering different levels of fear, the emergence of our "new brain" provided us with an essential counterbalance, which afforded us greater survival skills. As you can probably figure out, the name "cerebral cortex" reflects what it's designed to be—the "cerebral" part of us, our more reflective, analytical, rational, and logical part. The cerebral cortex comprises a number of important areas, including the prefrontal cortex, whose primary function is to balance out the impulses of the limbic brain. Like a CEO who orchestrates the many arms and functions of a company, the prefrontal cortex attempts to make sense out of these impulses, remove their absolute nature, and sort out whether a fear response is appropriate. Conversely, it also serves to modulate pleasure seeking. So we can see that the cerebral cortex functions became particularly important as we evolved as a species and developed civilizations and societies. By balancing out our basic drives, it allows us to function more adeptly within a world that is no longer black-and-white.

But preserving the balance between these two brains is not often easy. It turns out that this is not a two-way street, or a process in which each part of the brain gets equal billing. There are far more brain signals going from the old brain to the new brain than there are from the new brain to the old. As a result, the limbic brain is imbued with a greater power. This is likely due to the fact that this part of the brain evolved first and in a way that allows us to respond quickly to danger, without having to waste time processing danger signals. This was useful at one time, when danger was a large part of our lives. But now, as we know, it's much more rare. The consequence of this built-in favoritism, however, is that it gives the limbic response—and the survival instinct—a great deal of leverage, and an ability to bypass our more rational, thinking brain. This is why gut responses often take precedence over more reflective processes. It also explains why it's much more difficult for the cerebral brain to gain more control over the limbic brain. And, as you can imagine, this puts us more at the mercy of our survival instinct, which has come to be overreactive in our modern lives.

In addition, it's important to point out that since the limbic system has more direct connections to the sympathetic nervous system, its impulses can bypass the cerebral brain. This is why we can find ourselves reacting in a strong physical way even without being aware of any thoughts. Have you ever noticed, for example, that your heart is racing or that you are getting heated up or sweating without knowing why—only later to identify the source of your concern? It could relate to something that was said or even a certain smell or an old memory that was triggered. Notice that your visceral reaction *preceded* your awareness. So just these gut reactions become capable of eliciting a powerful physical response in the body.

Several studies have looked at how effective humans can be in regulating this limbic input. Some of the more interesting ones have examined the hunger response, which can radiate from the nucleus accumbens or the pleasure center in the limbic system. In one particular study, women were given a piece of desirable food. They were told to use cognitive techniques to control their limbic brain's response to the food. By forcing themselves to employ cognitive techniques, chiefly telling themselves that they should not be hungry or want the food, they were activating the prefrontal lobe of their cerebral cortex. The researchers then observed these women's brains through a functional PET scan and noticed that in fact their prefrontal lobes were activated. But that wasn't all that lit up on the screen. Their pleasure centers were activated as well. So even though the women were telling themselves they were not interested in the food, their limbic brains weren't buying it.

Other studies have looked at meditators to see how effective they could be in altering the limbic input. After all, if meditators can control their minds so well, then it would seem logical to assume they are better able to control their limbic responses. Interestingly, some studies have shown that experienced meditators can indeed influence limbic structures such as the amygdala, and other brain structures, such as the insular cortex, that attach meaning to physical sensations in the body. But even so, most of these studies prove that it takes quite a bit of experience in meditation to achieve such results and be able to fully regulate the limbic input.

Extreme Cases Point to Limbic Dominance

A great way to illustrate the limbic brain's overpowering quality is to consider post-traumatic stress disorder (PTSD), a condition we've heard a lot about lately with soldiers returning home from war in Iraq and Afghanistan. This disorder is the perfect example of what happens when the limbic system goes awry: The cortex becomes unable to manage and contain the limbic brain's sensitivity and input, and the individual is at the true mercy of the survival instinct. Scientists have looked into how these regions of the brain are affected by PTSD, and have found that veterans' cerebral brains are less effective at controlling the limbic side of things, leaving the limbic brain more firmly in charge and resulting in a lack of balance, or nonalignment.

A similar finding has been observed by a group of researchers led by Dr. Lisa Shin, of Tufts University, who noticed that people suffering from PTSD have an exaggerated amygdala response while also showing a diminished cerebral or prefrontal lobe response. Again, this means that these individuals have developed a condition in which their brains are less capable of dealing with situations that rely on the logical, rational, cerebral parts. Instead they are driven by their limbic side, which takes over the controls like a toddler behind the wheel of a car and provokes the survival instinct. The cerebral brain is practically paralyzed, unable to determine where the limbic brain is going.

Another example of limbic dominance is found in public speaking. When asked which is more frightening—public speaking or being diagnosed with cancer—many people would rather learn they have cancer than get up in front of a large group! And even though people know that their fear is irrational, they become immobilized at the idea of having to confront an audience. This may sound absurdly counterintuitive, but not when you consider that the fear of public speaking stirs up the issues of judgment, acceptance, and the possibility of rejection. Although it may not seem logical, the limbic brain interprets these types of feelings as there being a life-threatening emergency, leading the survival instinct to take action. These gut reactions are rooted strongly in the limbic brain, and this is an excellent example of how the limbic brain overrides the logical and reasoning part of the cerebral brain.

This also helps explain the odd, erratic, and often irrational behavior seen in extreme cases of PTSD. Last year, when the news reported on an American soldier who shot and killed seventeen Afghan civilians, including children, the media immediately began questioning whether PTSD was to blame. More could have been involved than just PTSD, and at this writing we still don't know what, exactly, transpired. But if we could have seen inside Staff Sergeant Robert Bales's brain during his shooting spree, it's quite possible that we would have witnessed a total shutdown of his cerebral side while his limbic brain, at the mercy of his survival instinct, held the firearms.

If your cerebral cortex cannot help manage the overly dramatic messages springing from your limbic system, you cannot effectively control your sense of fear or gauge the magnitude or seriousness of that fear. And this becomes the very basis of the survival instinct. As we continue to experience a chronic state of discomfort and fear, over time we may in fact destabilize the balancing system in place within the brain. This unfortunately leaves the limbic system in an activated state, while at the same time making us less and less in control of keeping it in check. The longer we sustain this elevated level of discomfort, the greater sensitivity we develop to it, and the more often our survival instinct is pressed into action. It ultimately takes less and less discomfort to spark a fear reaction and ignite the survival instinct. Thus, the more overreactive the limbic response becomes, the greater the role that the survival instinct and discomfort play in our lives, and the more control they exert on our behavior and our chemistry.

Another very important part of all this is that when the limbic system experiences fear and then triggers the sympathetic nervous system's fight-or-flight response, the trauma and fear that remain after the incident are even more encoded into the brain and body. This explains why traumatic experiences can lead to a dramatic change in someone's emotions and behavior. The brain and body evolved in such a way that these life-threatening situations would be remembered so that we could avoid them and be safer in the future. Unfortunately these encoded links between the limbic system and the sympathetic nervous system make these reactions very difficult to change or modify.

To bring another example into the picture, consider that you are flying home and experience extreme turbulence, which then provokes a significant amount of fear that is also inflamed by other passengers showing signs of concern and trepidation. This then creates a sympathetic response within you, and you may find that from that point on you become fearful of flying. It's like that old saying about getting back on the horse quickly if you fall off it: If you don't get over your fear of falling off a horse right away, you'll be fearful of horses and horseback riding forever. Fear reactions such as sheer panic or anxiety attacks are yet another perfect example of this. Anyone who has experienced a panic attack while driving on a busy freeway knows that it can be a challenge to get back on the highway again without fearing another panic attack in the same setting.

There is an old expression originally espoused by the late psychologist Donald Hebb: "That which fires together is that which becomes wired together." In other words, two things that happen at the same time become embedded within the brain together. So when two sets of neurons (brain cells) are triggered at the same time, even if they are totally separate events at first, the relationship between these two neural networks is now formed and they can become wired together—forever linked to one another and controlling all future firings of this now single set of conjoined neurons. This is how panic attacks can become forever connected to freeways or a certain food becomes associated with nausea. Therefore, if one of these events occurs in the future, it then triggers the neural network of the experience that's now been bonded with it.

Why does this happen? The fear that is experienced in such a setting can be so significant that it becomes attached to driving on the freeway in the future. In fact, it can begin to spread to other driving situations as well, from driving on a regular road to driving in your neighborhood. Even though it isn't logical to the cerebral brain, the limbic brain's survival instinct is now firmly in control, and as long as driving is connected to fear and danger—which to the limbic brain means potential death—it will avoid any hint of these situations in the future.

Is there a way to manipulate the conditioning of these "wired together" neural networks? A number of studies have determined that yes, it's possible to block the damaging effects of traumatic events and change how they are encoded within the limbic brain. In essence, there's a way to temper or even squelch the fear response. Medications such as beta blockers, which interfere with the sympathetic response, can achieve this, significantly reducing the traumatic experience, dampening the stress response, and helping the individual recover significantly quicker.

Our Genes Are at Stake

If it wasn't enough to be racked with fear from the survival instinct, there is growing data in the field of epigenetics that suggests that strong external influences such as fear can actually alter the expression of our genes. Epigenetics is a burgeoning field of study that examines changes in how our genes behave that are not related to alterations in DNA sequences. Although our DNA remains fixed and identical in all cells for our entire lives, there is now evidence to show that our genes don't act exactly the same in every cell. The same gene can express itself differently from one cell to the next, despite the same underlying DNA. These shifts in genetic expression can happen throughout our lives, depending on what we're exposed to in our environment. By "environment," I'm not referring just to classic sources of toxins and pollutants that can change our genes' functionality, but also to other forms of external "toxins" that can indeed affect our genetic expression. Child abuse, for example, which is characterized by trauma and fear, has been found to leave a profound epigenetic mark, strongly influencing how genes control the HPA axis, leaving these regions of the brain to react differently than they would otherwise.

What makes the subject of epigenetics particularly relevant to discomfort and the survival instinct is that the HPA axis of the brain is fiercely associated with the fight-or-flight response, which is the most obvious expression of the survival instinct. Considering this, we can see how chronic fear and discomfort might lead to genetic changes that would result in the survival instinct becoming overly sensitized. In addition to child abuse changing how individuals react to fear due to changes in their genes' expression, researchers have also discovered a potent connection between these changes and risk of suicide. As reported by phys.org, according to Canadian researchers Michael Meaney and Moshe Szyf at McGill University and the Douglas Institute in Quebec, "The function of our DNA is not as fixed as previously believed. The interaction between the environment and the DNA plays a crucial role in determining our resistance to stress thus the risk for suicide. Epigenetic marks are the product of this interaction." Hence, our inability to manage fear and discomfort can lead to serious consequences that can result in a significant alteration of our genes.

The point at which we're living in a chronic state of heightened limbic reactions is the point at which we're vulnerable to developing patterns, habits, and routines that attempt to manage these reactions, which leave us feeling out of control and overwhelmed. And without healthy strategies to manage our discomfort and the subsequent survival instinct, we begin to develop unhealthful strategies that have short-term value, can cause long-term harm, and have a profound effect on our health and our lives.

What kind of habits am I talking about? Those that are much more than an inconvenience or trite behavior. I'm referring to habits that prolong our sense of imbalance and the mismanagement of the limbic brain. These types of habits are much more insidious, and much more universal. In the following chapter, we'll discuss how we fall into unhealthy traps in our attempts to tame the ever so overreactive survival instinct.

Chapter 5

The Birth of a Bad Habit

Obsessions, Compulsions, and Addictions

We are all acquainted with habits. Most of us think of them in an innocuous way, such as washing your hands before eating or brushing your teeth at bedtime. Habits such as these are adaptive and serve a larger purpose. They can be daily rituals that simplify your life and free up other parts of the mind so you can focus and attend to other activities. Habits also have a survival value, as they can help us react in instantaneous ways. Quickly swerving your car to avoid a large object in the street and depressing the brake pedal when you need to stop suddenly are prime examples of this. Tasks such as these are automated, making it possible to handle these basic road functions as you contemplate more complex matters and thoughts.

There is a second class of habits, however, that are maladaptive and therefore "bad." These habits reflect a maladjustment in the world—a way of coping with the certain demands or stresses in ways that may not have positive, healthful outcomes. (For an outline of the most common types of bad habits, see the box on page 74.) Maladaptive habits and routines are formed when the limbic response becomes mismanaged, or, in more scientific terms, "dysregulated." They are emblematic of our attempt to manage those fearful feelings that emerge from the spiraling discomfort generated from deflated dopamine levels. The goal of these habits is a very primitive means of managing and distracting us from the fears stirred up by our internal instinct. Unfortunately, these types of habits do nothing to rid us of these fears. Instead they are merely short-term ploys to help us momentarily quell the fear. And as our dopamine reserves plummet, we are more likely to become ensnared within these patterns. In most cases, they accomplish this result by avoidance or distraction. Let me explain.

The Five Basic Types of Bad Habits

Maladaptive, "bad" habits are symptomatic of a hair-trigger survival instinct. They are essentially a way of creating makeshift safety, control, and comfort, but they can turn against us in health-depleting ways. The five most common types of maladaptive habits:

Addiction habits: overeating; abusing substances such as alcohol and drugs; excessive caffeine consumption (including energy drinks); overexercising; and sex addiction.

Compulsive habits: checking habits, compulsive organization and cleanliness (such as hand washing), hair pulling, and skin picking.

Sick habits: frequent colds and flu, headaches, chronic pain, stomachaches; a subset of this habit, which I'll explore later in the book, is the aforementioned Let Down Effect, whereby a person develops an illness or symptoms following a stressful event, such as a personal conflict, a time-pressured work project, or an exam.

Insomnia habit: inability to go to sleep and stay asleep.

Protective and avoidance habits: phobias designed to keep a person "safe" and free from harm; classic examples include fear of flying or enclosed spaces, leading a person to avoid airplanes or elevators. Pain can also be a protective habit whereby physical pain serves a purpose such as giving permission to escape or withdraw from normal responsibilities.

For starters, we'll take the example of Bethany, a high-level Hollywood agent. Over the past year and half, Bethany found herself becoming increasingly more keyed up due to a chronic state of agitance. Although work demands added to this feeling of being sped up all the time, she also felt it outside of work, in settings where it wasn't warranted. Eventually, Bethany's agitance levels crossed her discomfort threshold, and she began to notice signs of discomfort in the form of feeling abnormally anxious and temperamental. At first, she managed this discomfort with the use of herbal and vitamin supplements, such as valerian and GABA, which were intended to help calm her growing inner turmoil. But like the experience of so many other people, chronic states of discomfort create a growing vulnerability. It wasn't until she was returning home to California from the East Coast on a turbulent flight that her discomfort culminated in a maladaptive habit. Even though Bethany had experienced turbulence many times before in her travels, this time it was different. The combination of her underlying discomfort and the turbulence made for a Molotov cocktail. Her survival instinct awakened and caused her to feel like she was going to die in a plane crash. She knew it wasn't logical and even told herself that she'd been in situations like this before with no problem. But her logical mind wasn't listening as her limbic brain took control. She ordered several drinks in order to calm herself. Although this did help her make it through the flight, it did nothing to vanquish the fear that had established itself with regard to flying.

Bethany's job required frequent flying to meet clients around the country, so this responsibility began to pose a problem for her. Initially, she tried to overlook it, but her anxiety continued to progress with each anticipated trip. On some occasions, the anxiety was mild, but in others it was quite pronounced. Naturally this led to extraordinary distress at times, and it wasn't long before she began to seek a solution to cope with her fear of flying. First, she resorted to having a couple of drinks prior to boarding the plane, which provided some relief, but soon enough she was needing more drinks to assuage her dread. On one particular trip, while she was flying with a coworker, she felt embarrassed, particularly when her colleague mentioned to her that she appeared compromised by her dependence on alcohol.

After this incident, Bethany spoke with her family doctor, who prescribed antianxiety medication. This did indeed prove helpful and mitigated much of her anxiety on future flights. But as with alcohol, she came to rely on this medication, even taking it days in advance of a trip just so she could cope with thinking about the upcoming flight. She also began noticing that she would need higher and higher doses of medication just to get through flights. And to make matters worse, Bethany eventually tried to avoid plane trips altogether, canceling them at the last moment and making excuses to clients that she had become suddenly sick.

As you can see, Bethany's fear of flying led her to more than one maladaptive habit. In addition to her use of alcohol and then medications to contain her fear, she eventually avoided flying completely. While on the surface avoiding flying may not seem to be problematic or maladaptive, it is indeed maladaptive, because it reflects a growing defensiveness or guardedness in being in the world. The maladaptive habit, such as a reliance on medication, may have some success in curbing the fear at first, but it's not uncommon for it to lose its effective punch over time. At some point, total avoidance of a certain act or normal behavior becomes the only way to deal with the fear in an absolute, surefire way.

Once we begin to develop such habits to avoid fear, it begins to send shock waves into other aspects of our lives. This is what makes maladaptive habits so stealthy and far-reaching in their effects, as they can generalize or spread to other facets of an otherwise healthy life. Before long, Bethany was using her medication, which was originally prescribed for her just to be able to fly with ease, for all sorts of situations—from dealing with work stress to driving, riding on elevators, and relaxing before bedtime. This is also what makes maladaptive habits and chronic activation of the survival instinct so terribly problematic. They are like a flimsy veneer that is put up to serve as a shield against the fear—but it's made of straw and not steel, and is merely a false form of protection. Yet the more we resist confronting the fear and instead put up these defenses—the more we feed these unhealthy habits and routines—the greater the fear and the higher the level of discomfort. The bad habits themselves are enough to keep the discomfort button pressed, resulting in a permanent reliance on short-term solutions that act as loose bandages rather than real cures.

It's human nature to become fearful when we sense discomfort. But what tends to happen is that our fear can trigger our survival instinct, which then motivates us to take some form of action to feel safe again. That action can be a routine or habit that creates a faulty form of safety. But in reality it's a form of resistance against confronting the fear. And the more we resist, the greater our fear and discomfort become.

The maladaptive habits seemingly conceal the discomfort and the underlying survival instinct. But it grows like a cancer as it smolders within. In a sense, the bad habit is nothing more than a temporary distraction for our conscious mind. And at the same time, our cerebral mind finds ways to justify, rationalize, and overlook these habits while they are busy pilfering from and compromising our foundation of safety.

From Innocuous to Insidious

The example of Bethany is typical of so many different types of maladaptive habits, which tend to start in a fairly innocuous way but result in a full-blown encounter with the survival instinct. Initially, those rising levels of agitance go undetected until they exceed our threshold for discomfort, at which point we experience fear. The maladaptive habit is merely our human attempt to manage the pressing fear we feel in the moment. But the fear is so frightening and overwhelming to the survival instinct that it compels us to accept and try short-term solutions. In most cases these solutions are externally driven. In other words, we are turning to medication, alcohol, or avoidant behaviors to deal with the fear. So rather than learning to rely on or develop our own internal resources to manage the fear, we come to depend on these external forms of creating safety. Internal resources for managing fear include an inner strength and confidence, a hardiness, or a resilience. (We'll be exploring all the ways to build and harness these inner resources in part 2 of this book.)

As I've been describing, once the logical brain is at the mercy of our irrational, limbic brain, we're no longer effective in handling a situation that conjures our survival instinct and leads to unhealthy behaviors. Our cerebral brain cannot control or balance out the limbic response. No sooner do we become reliant on external forms of safety than we compromise our confidence even further. Rather than instilling safety, our fears rob us of our internal resources that would provide a permanent solution.

Put another way, our inner forms of managing fear begin to atrophy, and further erode the longer we continue to rely on external forms of safety. This is an important point, for even if we can mask our fear, it continues to reside within us, strengthening each time we engage in external solutions. It might help to think of all this in terms of a muscle. Once the limbic brain overtakes the cerebral brain thanks to our growing fears, our overly reactive survival instinct, and our dependence on external solutions, we're left with a weak, atrophied, and enfeebled cerebral brain that's chronically overpowered by its illogical counterpart.

In an earlier chapter I talked about Kate, who fell into the habit of overeating, relying on food as a way of managing her agitance and subsequent discomfort. Her story offered the perfect example of maladaptive habits arising with respect to overeating. Kate had a long history of overeating, starting somewhat harmlessly in college as she shouldered the demands of university life and increasing levels of discomfort related to class assignments, finals, and dating. Up until college, she had been a normal weight, but once she moved away and lived in the dorms, she became subject to dorm food and succumbed to the "freshman twenty." Within several years, food became her drug of choice to manage her agitance and discomfort. When she would feel uncomfortable, she found herself gravitating more and more toward food. Soon enough, a great discomfort emerged at the prospect of not being able to eat, and she found herself fearing getting hungry and not having any food available to quell her hunger.

For Kate, this was an incredibly powerful fear—a deep dread that something bad would happen if she couldn't eat at exactly the time she needed it. And once her survival instinct became involved in her eating response, even small amounts of discomfort were enough to trigger her eating addiction. Eventually, she found herself eating in anticipation of being hungry and uncomfortable. In other words, most of Kate's eating had nothing to do with being hungry—it was now a way to fend off the survival instinct. What makes this particularly challenging is that eating is how we are wired to survive. So when the survival instinct is triggered, we are drawn to food to ensure our survival. As long as Kate related the sensation of hunger to survival, she would be driven to eat. The act of eating may not seem like a bad or maladaptive habit, but in Kate's case it certainly was; clearly, using food in this manner was a short-term solution with a long-term destructive result: morbid obesity.

Kate gained control over her overeating by learning to detach the sensation and perception of hunger from the survival instinct. This opened the door for her to establish a more healthy relationship with food and see it for what it really is—fuel to live rather than a desperate attempt or a maladaptive habit to cope with an exaggerated or overly sensitized fear of discomfort.

Another example of how maladaptive habits can form from a relatively harmless experience is to consider the area of sleep once more. Or, more specifically, the task of falling asleep. More than fifty million prescriptions are filled annually for sleep medications. Clearly, the inability to fall sleep (and stay asleep) has become a large problem for millions of people. A small subset of these people have struggled with sleep their whole lives, but the vast majority of pill poppers today who struggle with insomnia developed this problem in their adulthood.

Will is a good example of this situation. He was a physician who had become accustomed to working long hours and getting home late. He frequently found himself doing computer work and returning e-mails right up to his late bedtime. As a result of this grueling schedule, habitual states of agitance pretty much came to define his workdays. While his work demands exacerbated his agitance, he felt perpetually activated, frustrated, and unable to complete his workload. He was, in a word, overwhelmed. Not surprisingly, Will would try to go to bed while in this state of mind, but be unable to switch his brain over to a relaxed, sleepy mode. Over time, it began to take hours for him to fall sleep, and the vicious cycle would commence: He'd go to bed late, fall asleep late, and wake up tired and fatigued, starting his day in an irritated state that further aggravated his agitance level all day long.

It wasn't long before Will's agitance levels became more and more piqued, leading to a growing discomfort and a concomitant fear that would greet him as he popped into bed each night. Eventually, he experienced the same domino effect we saw in Bethany—the chain of events that turned a relatively innocuous experience into an insidious habit. He began to fear the process of going to sleep, consumed by racing thoughts of not only his workload but also the torture of trying to fall asleep. This fear was the beginning of the survival instinct kicking in and being pressed into action. At first, Will turned to watching TV as a way to relax, and to distract himself from the going-to-bed thoughts, and even avoid the inevitable act of having to get into bed. But this in itself began to take its toll, as Will needed to keep the TV turned on for longer and longer periods so he could effectively downshift enough to go to sleep. And even though he would eventually fall sleep, he still would end up sacrificing quite a few hours and suffer exhaustion the next day. Just because he fell asleep didn't negate the fact he wasn't truly relaxed. In other words, the sleepy feeling overtook his feelings of discomfort enough to put him to bed but not enough to keep that discomfort from coming back the next day.

Will's futile means of coping—using the TV—and avoiding the process of going to bed was the genesis of his maladaptive habit. And like so many maladaptive habits, this one is generally ineffective in the long run. So it wasn't long before Will turned to sleep medications, which worked initially but ultimately pushed him down the slippery slope of needing heavier doses. In due course he found himself taking them on a regular basis, whether he truly needed them or not. The mere fear of insomnia, and the fear of not being able to perform the next day at work due to fatigue, was enough to keep his prescription filled and utilized. Because of this maladaptive habit, Will ultimately lost all faith in his own ability to fall sleep naturally. It was at this point that the limbic brain had fully taken control.

Before we look at one more example, let's review the sequence of events that I've outlined, starting with the initial agitating factor. Over time, this provides the fuel for discomfort and for establishing a maladaptive habit in hopes of extinguishing the fear. But, unfortunately, as we'll continue to see throughout this book, maladaptive habits have a way of compounding the problem and feeding a vicious cycle. The fear is never obliterated. The discomfort is never managed. And the original agitance still provides a sneaky source of endless fuel to the proverbial fire.

Lastly, let's consider Melissa, who suffers from irritable bowel. Melissa is someone whose agitance rose to a level at which it had an effect on her digestion. Specifically, her agitance interfered with and impaired her parasympathetic nervous system, which needs to operate well in order to digest food properly. The parasympathetic system is the body's counterbalance to the sympathetic system; while the sympathetic system is responsible for stimulating activities associated with the flight-or-fight response (i.e., ramping up the body's stress response), the parasympathetic nervous system controls activities when the body is at rest, including salivation, digestion, and defecation. The two systems aren't so much antagonistic as they are complementary—the sympathetic system is all about quick responses whereas the parasympathetic system

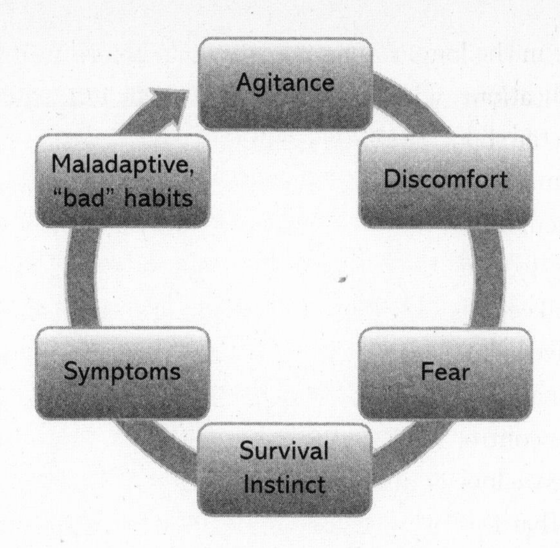

commands actions that don't require such immediate reactions. In Melissa's case, over time her eating and digestion became associated with a sympathetic response instead of a parasympathetic response. It wasn't long before this disruption in her parasympathetic system led to intestinal cramping, bloating, and frequent trips to the bathroom even when she hadn't eaten. Eventually Melissa found herself feeling more and more discomfort with lower and lower levels of agitance. Additionally, even low-level stressful moments such as rushing to an appointment, being caught in traffic, or encountering an unexpected frustration would trigger her intestinal discomfort. Soon enough, Melissa came to fear her GI disturbances, especially worrying that they'd arise during inopportune times, such as while driving, flying, in meetings, or in other public places. As expected, her survival instinct awakened to this rising discomfort. When she felt there was no available bathroom or that she'd begin to feel stomach pain when there was "no way out," Melissa's survival instinct would foment a massive panic reaction, fanning the flames of her stomach pain and symptoms of IBS. This cycle of fear and symptoms would only grow bigger and more ferocious, creating the foundation for maladaptive habits to form. For Melissa, this meant avoiding places that lacked readily accessible bathrooms, taking routes to work where there were bathrooms along the way, refusing to schedule meetings in the morning, and shunning certain foods or stressful situations.

While all of these examples showcase different problems and very distinct consequences to each individual, they all share one common and powerful feature: a pathway from an initial, seemingly harmless state of agitance to the establishment of a bad habit sprung from a well-defined interplay of discomfort, fear, survivalist reactions, and physical symptoms. Each of these people may have had wildly different agitance to start, but for all of them it ultimately culminated in maxing out their individual tolerance for discomfort, setting in motion a cascade of events.

The development of bad habits as I have described can occur in very blatant ways. But at other times they can arise much more subtly, through a very powerful but stealthy form of conditioning. In the following chapter I will give an overview of how conditioning can contribute to the cementing and shaping of our habits, allowing them to take an increasingly larger role in our lives.

Chapter 6

Conditioning and the Genesis of Habits

Please and Thank You

Most of us are unaware of how conditioned our behavior, thoughts, and feelings are. We are creatures of habit, whether it's what we eat for breakfast each day, the need to have a pastry and newspaper with our coffee, driving the same route to work, or even waking up at the same time in the middle of the night. We take all this for granted, or at least we don't stop to think about how ingrained these behaviors are, many of which contribute to our health and wellness. But we should consider how this very same conditioning affects so many other aspects of our lives, such as when we catch a cold, gain weight, or develop a headache. Some of these we can live with and others are not only invasive but can be seriously detrimental to our well-being.

It should come as no surprise that over time, our maladaptive habits become less and less effective. They can feel like they are warding off the awakening of the survival instinct, but they are incredibly deceptive. We may think we are controlling the threat, but in reality we are giving up more and more ground to it as it spreads like wildfire within us, usurping the control and resources we have left. In more extreme cases, we are fleeced of our inner resources, and catapulted into a state of feeling out of control. We are left face-to-face with the survival instinct, with little at our disposal to manage it. It is at this point we have hit bottom and have fallen into a state of what I call Conditioned Powerlessness. We become virtually immobilized by the survival instinct, which can become the genesis of major mental and physical illness.

First, let's get this definition straight. By "conditioning," I'm referring to the act of becoming trained or accustomed to something such that it's automatic or effortless. In a purely physical sense, for instance, we can condition our bodies to lift twenty-pound weights easily or run a mile in under ten minutes. But conditioning goes much further than that. Much in the way we can condition the body physically, we can also condition ourselves to think, behave, or feel a certain way. We can condition our bodies down to the cellular level, where we can have an impact on how our bodies respond to stress or even handle a germy invader. And it's these types of conditioning that we are concerned with. As this chapter is about to reveal, conditioning strongly influences the types of habits we form as a result of agitance and discomfort. When we fall prey to our survival instinct, we can develop habits to cope with that uncomfortable feeling of having the inner survivalist on alert. In this cascade of events, the body's natural conditioning processes then shape those habits and dictate how influential and powerful they become in our lives—for better or worse.

Although there may be times when we are mindful of our conditioning, in most cases it generally escapes our awareness. For example, many of us have been well trained to say "thank you" after someone does us a favor or "excuse me" if we need someone to get out of our way. Over time, and with experience, we become conditioned to operate a car without needing to think through every step. For another example, consider what happens when you see another person yawning. You might find yourself yawning in response and even feel sleepy. In this case, a mere visual cue has the ability to elicit a physical reaction within us. In all of these commonplace examples, we have no conscious awareness of our thoughts the moment we say "pardon me," press the brake pedal, or yawn.

Many people mistakenly assume that awareness precedes most thoughts that govern behavior. But it's actually quite the reverse—most of our reactions to the world are automatic reflexes. Perhaps the most striking and ultimately significant form of conditioning relates to our health, which is dramatically affected by the profound conditioning that typically occurs when we are unaware of it. I'll be getting to the details of this phenomenon shortly. For now, let's turn our attention to the broader concept of conditioning.

Types of Conditioning

Technically speaking, conditioning occurs when there is a pairing of two different things that have no relationship per se, but by virtue of their pairing come to have a relationship and meaning. Let's consider a classic example: learning not to touch a hot stove. Before you experienced the burn of touching a hot stove or oven, you didn't know about the relationship between a hot stove and a bad burn. But in one trial of learning, you no doubt learned this relationship rather quickly (and painfully!). In the future you knew to keep your hands away from all things that are hot. The moment we first burn ourselves, we become conditioned to associate the sensation of pain with a hot stove. We also learn this in the realm of food. If we find that spicy food such as curry or jalapenos makes us sick, from that point on we avoid dishes with those ingredients.

There are actually two types of conditioning. One you probably heard about in high school biology class when your teacher talked about Pavlov's dogs. Ivan Pavlov, a Russian physiologist, was the first to experiment with and document conditioning, more than a century ago. His work has led to a rich body of research attesting to the power of conditioning and its scientific validity. In the late nineteenth century, Pavlov noticed that before he gave his dogs red meat, they began to salivate. Probing deeper into this "psychic secretion," as he called it, he then began to ring a bell prior to bringing out the red meat. Soon the mere ringing of the bell triggered the dogs' salivation. This salivation in response to the bell was a passive reflex, or an autonomic response by the dogs' bodies; today we call this the conditioned response or conditional reflex. Pavlov would spend the majority of his life committed to the study of physiology and neurology, especially as these areas pertained to the digestive system.

The second type of conditioning, called operant or instrumental conditioning, was made famous by Burrhus Frederic (B. F.) Skinner in the twentieth century. This type of conditioning is related to learning a certain behavior by creating an association to affect that behavior. The best way to understand this is to consider a common scenario: If you're trying to get a child to make her bed more often, you reward her every time she does it, such as by giving her money or points toward a toy she wants. Reinforcing the behavior with a reward every time the child makes the bed typically translates to her making her bed more frequently. She is becoming *instrumentally* conditioned to make the bed routinely.

Although Pavlovian and Skinnerian conditioning reflect the chief types of conditioning, from these we get numerous subtypes that can influence us in profound ways, and that may seem more relevant to our everyday lives. Let's take a quick tour.

PAIRING

Pairing is the first subtype of conditioning that can influence maladaptive habits. Pairing occurs when two unrelated activities, experiences, situations, or internal events form a causal relationship. Let me give you a personal example. My first job out of graduate school was running an alcohol treatment program for the Veterans Administration in Los Angeles. On a daily basis, I would hear alcoholic patients lament that a drink would help them deal with their stress and frustrations in life. Then one day when I was driving home through the thick and unrelenting Southern California traffic (all commuters know how uncomfortable this can feel), a thought crept into my mind that went like this: "Man, I can't wait to get home and grab a beer out of the refrigerator." The absurdity of this thought was that I don't even like beer and never have it in my kitchen. Plus, I didn't come from an alcoholic home, so I didn't grow up with these types of messages. But after hearing statements like this over and over, the compulsion and the idea that the way to manage my discomfort was to reach for alcohol had now sunk in and had become part of me. If I hadn't been someone who was tuned in to mind traps, I might have looked for a liquor store on the way home, and this would have surely sealed within me the pairing of alcohol with the release of stress or fatigue.

Advertising companies are very successful at using this type of conditioning to shape our maladaptive habits. Commercials similarly show people drinking alcohol and engaging in fun activities. In your mind, you start to create a link between two otherwise separate events. The cigarette industry has been very clever in this regard, for the Marlboro Man embodies so many attributes people admire. The link that many of us have ingrained in our heads from all those advertisements is that if you smoke Marlboro cigarettes, then you'll feel rugged, sexy, attractive, and in control. And for those individuals who are developing maladaptive habits, smoking can become a way of managing their discomfort and survival instinct. Even though smoking is a maladaptive means of coping, the cigarette industry has given it a positive spin in which smokers unconsciously feel resilient and in control.

In an earlier chapter I described how Andrea was attending a work function back east and suddenly felt fearful while in a hot and stuffy room. From that moment on, there was a relationship for her between hot and stuffy settings and feelings of fear. In actuality, though, her fear was a function of uncontrolled agitance building up and a subsequent growing discomfort, which culminated in a survivalist response coinciding with being in a hot and stuffy room. This firmly rooted her maladaptive habit of avoidance that revolved around the issue of heat, stuffiness, and lack of adequate air-conditioning—another classic case of pairing.

GENERALIZATION

The second subtype of conditioning is called generalization, and it's very similar to pairing. In generalization, the habit begins to spread, or generalize, to other conditions or situations that had no previous relationship with it. The advertising companies may take a maladaptive habit such as overeating and then expand it to another maladaptive habit, such as the consumption of alcohol. Because maladaptive habits are built on fear, they are highly susceptible to conditioning, so they are an easy target for generalization. And since food and alcohol influence the pleasure center of the limbic system, the connection between them becomes even more cemented and dangerous. Again, the clinical case of Andrea also reflects this type of conditioning, as she began associating a hot and stuffy room with fearfulness and feelings of being trapped or suffocated. It wasn't long before she developed extreme claustrophobia in crowded places, which gave her the feeling that she could not escape quickly enough if the suffocating feeling struck. Over time, she began to avoid congested places altogether because she had generalized her one-time experience in that hot and stuffy room to virtually all settings that had an inkling of similar characteristics.

Another example of generalization comes from my own life again, but from long ago. In 1977, as a second-year graduate student, I noticed that my hands and fingers were developing sores and cuts on them that wouldn't heal quickly. Initially, I attributed the condition to playing tennis five times a week, as well as playing guitar in clubs several nights a week to pay my rent and food bills. But then I noticed that my fingers were aggravated just by washing my hands with soap and water. My skin condition continued to deteriorate, and it wasn't long before my fingerprints were barely detectable. (I knew this because I was fingerprinted at the DMV and the clerk kept asking me to push harder on the pad because there were only traces of fingerprints left on my hands.) Not only did this condition begin to hamper my tennis and music, but it was like I was carrying a sign over my head letting others know that I was defective. It gave me a great appreciation for others who suffer from visible conditions.

Naturally, I sought out dermatologists in my university's medical school, and I learned that I had eczema, and that it had many causes. The only cure was to continue with the customary steroid salves, which were temporary fixes. Later, I started to wonder if an allergy could be to blame, because I noticed that when I visited a girlfriend in another city, miraculously my skin would get better. Then when I was reading a textbook on psychopathology I came across an article about eczema being psychosomatic. *Was I doing this to myself?* As a graduate student studying to be an expert in this area, I thought I was above this type of thing, but clearly I wasn't. A condition is called psychosomatic when there is a real physical problem that is influenced by nonphysical elements, such as emotions or stress. Now things began to make sense: I felt better when I was away because it was associated with pleasure and fun; on the other hand, home was associated with work and school.

Conditions such as eczema and psoriasis can arise due to a genetic predisposition. But they can also be triggered by certain physical situations, such as, in my case, too much wear and tear on my skin, or in other cases, chemicals that come in contact with the skin. It is not, however, uncommon for these conditions to be precipitated initially by periods of great stress or emotion.

Initially, the affliction is triggered by the same situation—a specific allergy, a particular stressor, etc. But after a while, generalization can begin to set in, whereby other triggers that are not part of the initial cause of the skin's reactions begin to set it off. So in my case, it began with wearing down my hands with tennis and guitar playing. Eventually, stress became capable of causing the symptoms, and eventually nonstressful situations, such as waiting to catch the bus or the prospect of asking a girl out for a date, could cause them as well.

SUBLIMINAL CONDITIONING

The third subtype, subliminal conditioning, is one of the more interesting, but perhaps most scary, means of influencing maladaptive habits. In subliminal conditioning, we can be influenced without our conscious awareness. In other words, we can find ourselves acting in certain ways without knowing why we are responding in this manner.

Subliminal refers to a stimulus that occurs outside our conscious awareness. It does not mean that we don't actually hear or see the stimulus. Rather, it implies that although it may be discernible, we just overlook it. There are different types of subliminal conditioning, the most common of which are visual and auditory forms. Auditory subliminal conditioning and visual subliminal conditioning can have a profound effect on the brain and behavior.

One of my first experiences of visual subliminal conditioning was in high school, when I learned that if I nodded my head consistently while my teacher was talking (and while fellow students sat passively), I could condition her to direct her attention primarily to me.

Later, as a grad student, I used a form of tactile subliminal conditioning. At the time, I was dating a girl who liked to drive too fast for my comfort level. My verbal pleas to her to drive slower only led to endless arguments. But I learned that if I massaged her neck when she drove too quickly, she'd lighten up on the accelerator. I ultimately found that this was a much better way to encourage safer driving and avoid arguments.

Much later in my life, I had to use subliminal conditioning again to shape my kids' sleeping behavior. As many parents know, it can be quite a challenge to get kids ready for sleep and to accept bedtime. For many parents, the long, drawn-out process is rife with unnecessary conflict and stress—certainly the last thing we want to associate with sleep. So what I did to solve this problem was every time I saw my kids starting to get sleepy, for example, falling asleep in the car, I would begin to sing a certain song. Later, whenever I wanted my kids to begin shifting to a slower rhythm that would make it easier for them to sleep, I would sing the song. Sometimes I would hum the song while they were doing other things, helping them slow down even when they were involved in something more active. Once the subliminal conditioning was established, I would sing this song at bedtime to help them let go and give in to the sleepy feeling. For years my kids would ask me to sing the song so they could fall sleep more easily.

One of the first studies to analyze subliminal conditioning in a scientific setting was conducted by Duke University's Grainne M. Fitzsimons, Tanya L. Chartrand, and Gavan J. Fitzsimons in 2008. These researchers performed a most interesting experiment in which they subliminally showed the Apple logo to a group of people and the IBM logo to another group. When both groups were then asked to complete a standard laboratory task, those who had seen the Apple logo were more creative than those who took in the IBM logo. Did exposure to the Apple logo, which implies the company's "think different" brand and image, cause this difference? That's what these researchers concluded. They also played with the Disney Channel logo versus the E! Channel logo, finding that people who were exposed to the iconic symbol of Mickey Mouse were the more honest and sincere of the two groups. In 2010, University of Toronto researchers Chen-Bo Zhong and Nina Mazar took this kind of experiment further when they showed that exposure to products branded as "green" led people to act more altruistically than those who just viewed regular products. (However, they also found that people act *less* charitable and are more likely to cheat and steal after purchasing green products than after buying conventional ones! A possible explanation for this is that buying green products makes people feel like they've done enough good and can now act less moral.)

Perhaps some of the most striking examples of how subliminal stimulation influences health is in the area of eating. A number of interesting studies published in the past few years have uncovered fascinating relationships between fast food symbols and decision making. One set of studies, performed by Chen-Bo Zhong and Sanford E. DeVoe, involved the subliminal flashing of six well-known fast food logos to a group of people. Another group, which served as the control, was shown neutral images. The result? Our behaviors can indeed change when we're exposed to symbols of fast food, particularly behaviors involving speed, efficiency, and impulsivity. Zhong and DeVoe discovered that the subliminal logo group showed a strong preference for time-saving products, as they rated items such as two-in-one shampoo, three-in-one skin care solution, and high-efficiency detergent more positively than the control group. They also showed a preference for these quick-and-easy products over their original, "regular" versions. Then the researchers took this experiment further, delving into the topic of money. They asked both groups to choose between a small amount of money now or a larger amount of money in a week—a classic way to test the need for instant gratification. As you might have guessed by now, the subliminal fast food logo subjects were more likely to prefer the smaller payment now rather than wait for the larger payoff. Interestingly enough, the researchers also determined that the subliminal fast food logo group could read much faster on average. Zhong and DeVoe's paper, published in *Psychological Science*, is just one example among many studies that highlight the various ways in which everyday encounters with different brands and products can subtly and somewhat unconsciously influence our behavior.

Clearly, in addition to the emergence of fast food leading to a great need for instant gratification, it's also caused people to change certain aspects of their behavior that make them more impulsive. This makes sense when you think about it. Unlike traditional dining, fast food allows us to obtain our meals relatively quickly. The entire experience is one of speed, so anything associated with speed, such as impulsiveness and impatience, becomes part of the picture. The effect of this is that the mere symbols of fast food—whether it's the golden arches of McDonald's or the image of Colonel Sanders of KFC—can result in impatient, impulsive behavior, which can then trigger behaviors like overeating. This partly explains why these researchers also noted a strong relationship between fast food symbols and people's ability to feel happiness. Not only did the subjects choose short-term goals over long-term goals, but they also found it more difficult to experience joy. Once food becomes associated with speed, we can become conditioned to eat faster and consume more than we really need.

Research has also demonstrated that overeating can be strongly influenced by subliminal messages of fear of abandonment; if you have unresolved issues from abandonment or are highly sensitive to rejection (and thus fear of abandonment), you could use food to create the comfort you crave to stave off those fears. In studies in which this fear can be controlled, the overeating can also be brought under control. Other research has revealed how background music influences food and alcohol consumption as well: Music makes us eat quickly, and fast music causes fast drinking. What's more, research has shown how thirst-related words or smiling faces can subliminally increase viewers' thirst and subsequently how much they drink (just think of the latest soda pop commercial).

Subliminal conditioning isn't just about the outside world influencing us; we are also constantly influencing how other people feel and react. As parents, for instance, we can predispose children with our messages and conditioning to get sick, stay sick, or develop fearful reactions to the world. One of the most notable examples of this is how parents who suffer from sleeping problems may inadvertently condition their children to have fears and anxiety about sleep. In another example, it's been shown that what we see in other people's behavior involving food, such as what they choose to eat and how much they consume, can have profound subliminal effects on our own choices.

All of this research goes to show just how influential subliminal messaging can be on our behaviors—despite the notion of free will. No doubt this form of conditioning can strongly influence the magnitude and crystallization of our maladaptive habits.

As we just saw, this is particularly true with respect to overeating and excessive drinking. These two behaviors are powerfully influenced by the limbic brain's pleasure center. And we can see how, as long as this subliminal conditioning can directly act on the limbic brain, it could influence our fear reactions and levels of discomfort, ultimately causing us to make choices that are harmful as these maladaptive habits form.

STATE-DEPENDENT LEARNING

The fourth subtype of conditioning is called state-dependent learning, which can be best understood in this way: The state in which we learn something is the state in which we are best able to recall it. This type of conditioning can often fuel habits that are sustained by circumstances we think are out of our control. Experiencing "white coat phenomenon" is a classic example of this kind of conditioning. This isn't really a phenomenon at all—it's a bona fide syndrome in which patients show elevated blood pressure due to their anxiety about being in a doctor's office, where there's a chance the doctor will find something wrong with them. Their anxiety crystallizes as high blood pressure, which then becomes associated with the doctor and this particular setting. People who experience this "phenomenon" have become conditioned to respond this way every time they enter their physician's office.

Several years ago a professional football player was sent to me after finishing rehab for a back injury he received when he was struck by a defensive player while making an airborne catch. Long after his physical injury had healed, he was still experiencing pain each time he went out for a pass during a game, despite feeling no pain during practice and off the field. It was as if his body was anticipating being hit and getting injured again; his pain experience was now associated with playing football. Nothing was physically wrong with him, but his body learned—and remembered—the symptom even though there was no longer an underlying physical problem.

State-dependent learning primarily has been applied to basic learning. For example, in one study, those people who memorized words after an alcoholic drink could best recall the words several weeks later when they were given a drink again, versus those who were not served a drink.

I have found that state-dependent learning is a major player with respect to health and habits. Early in my career, I worked with a business executive who smoked exclusively in hotel rooms while traveling on business. Because his wife disapproved of his smoking, he had convinced her that he'd quit. But when he was away from home, he acted out his hidden desire to smoke, like a child getting away with something when his parents were gone. Over time, hotel rooms independently became associated with smoking so that the moment he stepped into a hotel room on a business trip, he'd light up—a clear case of state-dependent conditioning. It became evident from meetings with him that his smoking reflected an old rebelliousness forged in his youth, related to his Mennonite upbringing. Now both hotel rooms and his rebelliousness became triggers for smoking. I didn't have time to resolve his repressed anger and rebelliousness and his unhealthy state-dependent learning before he was set to go on another business trip, and he asked me if I could find a short-term solution for this behavior in the meantime. With hypnosis, I decided to supplant his desire to smoke in a hotel room by conditioning the hotel room and his rebelliousness to a different outcome. I suggested to him that when he was struck with the desire to rebel by smoking, he would feel distracted by a sudden urge to stuff a hotel towel in his suitcase. And it worked. The next time I saw him, he reported that he didn't smoke while away, but that he arrived home with a suitcase filled with hotel towels. He stated to me, "I think you may have something to do with this!" After removing this suggestion, I was able to finish working with him to recondition his maladaptive habit and change his harmful state-dependent learning.

State-dependent learning can influence health in other ways, too. One particular example that I have seen relates to those who have experienced seasonal affective disorder, sometimes called SAD. These individuals experience depression during the fall and winter months, when there is less daylight and exposure to the sun. Part of the physiological explanation for this is the light's influence on neurotransmitters in the brain—the lack of light during the fall and winter causes changes in the brain's chemistry to bring on feelings of depression. What makes this condition most interesting, however, is that when these individuals move to southern states where sunlight is plentiful throughout the year, many of them still experience this SAD response. This is a good demonstration of how certain times of the year have now become associated with precipitating an emotional response even when there is no physical basis for it.

It's well documented that acute episodes of stress can lead to illness. But if stress leads to illness, then you would expect that people would always become sick *during* the stressful period. Yet, many people become sick or develop physical symptoms, which can include panic attacks, *after the stressful period is over* (when they least expect it)—at a point when they are actually beginning to relax. This explains why some people get sick on vacation or following events that are stressful, or develop serious, sometimes fatal illnesses soon after retiring. Ironically, the biochemistry of de-stressing can play a role in becoming ill. Part of my life's work has been the investigation of what I call the Let Down Effect, which was chronicled in 2001 in my first book, *When Relaxation Is Hazardous to Your Health*, and proposes the idea that, as the book's title suggests, sudden relaxation can actually be unhealthy at times. I coined the term the *Let Down Effect* to describe the condition that occurs when a person develops an illness or symptoms following stressful events, such as a conflict, a time-pressured work project, or school exams. It can even occur after positive events, such as a wedding or a sports event, and frequently happens during or after weekends, holidays, vacations, or retirement. It's important to note that these illnesses are not imagined but are actually very real.

There is one particular type of let down, in which people who don't manage their agitance, discomfort, and stress levels effectively eventually develop the maladaptive habit of becoming sick after certain extended periods of agitance and discomfort. And with each let down in this situation, shorter periods and lower amounts of agitance, discomfort, and stress become capable of creating a Let Down Effect. After a period of time in which this pattern has occurred, situations of even moderate agitance, discomfort, or stress become the state-dependent condition to elicit the Let Down Effect. Further, eventually certain times of the year or events also become encoded within the state-dependent learning. One of the most common that I've seen is what I call the "postholiday blues" or "postholiday illnesses." These individuals become habituated to getting sick after Christmas or New Year's.

So we can see that state-dependent learning can affect us all the way down to our biochemistry and cell response. Put simply, our immune system can learn to "let us down" during certain circumstances because in the past those situations have been associated with a compromised immune response. And once we become consciously aware of our body developing this kind of symptom ("I always get sick while on vacation!"), the brain develops a neural network to precipitate the sickness as well. This means that our thoughts become capable of influencing illnesses or symptoms by triggering the series of biochemical events that lead to illness.

The Let Down Effect has far-reaching implications. It can influence a medley of health challenges, including the common cold, influenza (seasonal and H1N1), depression and anxiety, headaches, stomach pain, panic attacks, binge eating, skin outbreaks, allergic reactions, and exhaustion.

Another example of state-dependent learning is something I have seen in migraine patients, for whom certain conditions, such as work, weekends, certain smells, air-conditioning, or family dynamics, become associated with getting migraines. Over time, just the *anticipation* of these situations can precipitate a migraine. I've also watched this state-dependent learning take hold of people who condition themselves to wake up in the morning with physical symptoms, such as a stomachache, jaw pain, and headaches. For these people, state-dependent learning has created an association between waking up in the morning and annoying and disabling symptoms.

I'll give one more example of state-dependent learning, this one from my experience at the Veterans Administration's alcohol treatment program during my first job. Many of the alcoholics I treated were from skid row or had otherwise fallen through the different layers of society to find themselves stripped of virtually everything. A large subset of these veterans would sustain a level of sobriety for three months, only to have a desperate need to go on a drinking spree, before getting sober again. As I began to identify this three-month pattern of sobriety followed by bingeing, I wondered if it was a form of state-dependent learning whereby three months of sobriety became associated with having a binge. To test out my theory, I decided to use hypnosis on these individuals just prior to their reaching a three-month period of sobriety, and under hypnosis suggest to them that they were going through a binge. I would bring them through all the agonizing parts of the binge, the physical and emotional discomfort, and then to the eventual desire to become sober again. This ultimately allowed these veterans to circumvent having a binge just so they could return to sobriety. The three-month period became reconditioned with sobriety rather than with another binge.

ASSOCIATION

Association is the final form of conditioning. This type of conditioning, which is particularly influenced by film and TV, occurs when a certain emotional or physical state becomes associated with a course of action. One of the best examples of this can be found in television programs or movies in which a conflict between two or more people is portrayed and one person is obviously agitated or upset. The camera then shows that this individual has to leave the room or reach for a glass of alcohol or light up a cigarette. Hence, the message in the film or TV show is that it's unsafe to feel this type of agitation or conflict, and the only way to manage it is to drink alcohol, light up a cigarette, or flee the situation. It's no surprise that we as a culture come to fear discomfort, let alone situations in which the survival instinct becomes triggered.

Conditioning at the Cellular Level: The Inflammatory Link

The conditioning of maladaptive habits isn't just relegated to thoughts, behaviors, and symptoms. It can actually occur at a more primary level—at the cellular and biochemical level. This may be the most insidious form of conditioning of all, because most of it may go unnoticed for years, and won't surface until it erupts and morphs into something substantial or catastrophic.

Most types of cellular conditioning serve a valuable purpose; specific cells of the body are conditioned and trained to attack and neutralize bacteria and pathogens that the body considers a threat. These cells are called antibodies, which are programmed to multiply and then attack very specific threats. Antibodies are very clever in that they are specifically designed to target a very small invader, such as a single cell or one bacterium. In other words, they can condition themselves to deal with a particular antagonist invading the body, and in doing so, eradicate the threat. It's adaptation in action. In most cases, this process is a lifesaver and survivalism at its best. But over time, these conditioned cells can become a little too zealous in their goals, and when there is no actual threat and no battle to fight, they create one—instead of attacking pesky invaders, they begin attacking organs of the body. This is the cause of autoimmune disorders, such as type 1 diabetes, hyperthyroidism, rheumatoid arthritis, lupus, and ulcerative colitis. These autoimmune soldiers become what is known as "inflammatory." There are far more soldiers than what is truly needed in one place, and they create an inflammatory condition, just as if you had too many drunken sports fanatics congregated in one place who are all rooting for their own team to win. It's tumultuous and potentially flammable.

The concept of inflammation, which is becoming a household word for many Americans, currently dominates the field of aging and disease. When we think of inflammation, we may picture a swollen, sprained ankle or an itchy mosquito bite that is visibly inflamed and irritated from scratching. Yet inflammation is actually a ubiquitous process within the body. It's a mechanism the body depends on to facilitate healing.

In a nutshell, inflammation is a means of shoring up the body's defenses against attack—whether it's an infection, a cut finger, or a sore throat. The body creates inflammation to boost its cells and ward off illness or infection. So the intentions of inflammation are salubrious. But as we age or are confronted with chronic stress and the resulting agitance and discomfort, the amount of inflammation produced in the body exceeds our actual demands. In a sense, our body loses its natural checks and balances, and as a result, we find that the inflammatory response, like our antibodies, begins to run amok without any true enemy to target. Now, rather than finding invading viruses or physical assaults, it tenaciously begins to weaken the very cells and tissues it was meant to protect. This internal civil war wears down our natural defenses, predisposing us to disease and accelerating the aging process. The end result of chronic inflammation is well documented, and is associated with nearly every major illness, from heart disease and some forms of cancer to Alzheimer's, arthritis, autoimmune disorders, chronic pain, and allergies.

One of the earliest studies demonstrating how the inflammatory process can be conditioned was published in the journal *Science* in 1982, when scientists discovered that they could condition the inflammatory response in rats in such a way as to automatically change their immune system. Rats were first given a medication that suppressed their immune system's inflammatory response, paired with sugar-flavored water. The rats kept drinking the sugary water, which continued to suppress their immune system and inflammatory response. Eventually, the scientists removed the actual suppressor but allowed the rats to continue drinking sweet water. What happened? The rats still showed a dampened immune system and reduced inflammatory response. Bear in mind that this change occurred at the cellular level without requiring some form of complex reasoning like that found in our human cerebral cortex. Since that study, others have emerged to suggest a remarkable conclusion: If our cells—the very building blocks of our body—can be trained outside of the reach of our cerebral awareness, then virtually any process in the body can be trained to operate a certain way.

Prior to beginning a study on stress and inflammation years

ago, I wanted to see if I could influence the inflammation in my body through my own mind-body techniques. With the help of a local biomedical laboratory, I took a series of blood tests under different conditions—during a typical workday, following exercise, prior to eating a meal, and so on—and charted my varying levels of cytokines. Briefly, cytokines are proteins that are the antecedent of the inflammatory response. They can be an excellent barometer of the negative effects stress has on the body. Cytokines act as chemical messengers, telling other cells to activate, grow, or even die. Although they regulate the immune system responses and can drive the inflammatory process for positive outcomes, they can also perpetuate a chronic inflammatory process that goes unchecked. Put simply, high levels of inflammatory cytokines when you're not sick or enduring life-threatening stress reflect an unhealthy level of chronic inflammation, which is correlated with a number of conditions and diseases.

My cytokine numbers were generally squeaky clean, with the exception of one morning after a night of sleep interrupted by my barking dog, howling coyotes, and my young son, who was sick and needing attention. At breakfast, I was exhausted and irritable, and dreading the rigors of my upcoming day, which included two hours of teaching, eight hours of patients, and a two-hour presentation to give that night. To say I was cranky before the day even began and that my agitance levels were up is an understatement. And the effects of this on my body were clearly evident in the blood I drew that morning: My cytokine levels had shot well outside the "normal" range, indicating that my body was besieged by inflammation that I couldn't necessarily feel but that was festering deep within. My immune system had been needlessly put on alert, as if geared for battle (which you could argue I was, given my busy agenda for the day).

My personal experiment demonstrates how seemingly normal, everyday events can lead to insidious inflammatory changes in the body. When days like the one I had are few and far between, then it's hardly consequential—no more than eating a bacon cheeseburger once in a while is harmful to our waistlines. But if we become accustomed to a pattern of habits that mismanage our survival instinct, then what we find is that we are programming our bodies to sustain massively destructive levels of inflammation. And this is arguably one of the most detrimental ramifications of a survival instinct run amok, as it ultimately changes how fast we age.

Rethink, Retrain

Clearly, our conditioning strongly predisposes us to different moods, various health conditions, certain behaviors, and much more. I noticed that when I turned fifty, all of a sudden I became much more prone to colds and flu, finding myself sick multiple times during the year. When I stopped to think about why this was happening, I realized that I believed such an age represented a turning point in my life. Somewhere in my mind I thought that turning fifty would entail more illness, more degenerative conditions as I continued to age. And lo and behold, that toxic belief made me much more vulnerable to illness—illness that I would typically be able to resist. This may sound absurd on some level, for certain illnesses *are* caused by germs and uncontrollable pathogens. But take a moment just to think about friends and family members in your own life who, once they were diagnosed with an illness, seemed to surrender to it quickly, dying much sooner than they would have if they had not known they were sick. It's as if they became resigned to the ultimate totality—and fatality—of their diagnosis, ultimately giving up the fight. Anyone who has ever witnessed a loved one dying knows the power of thoughts in those final days and hours. Indeed, the power of conditioning is so great that we cannot overlook it, for it can factor into how fast we age and when we die.

In this chapter I have reviewed how different forms of conditioning have a strong impact on our maladaptive habits. Although they may not be the cause of a habit, they certainly do affect its magnitude and shape. Perhaps the most frightening part of how this conditioning influences our habits is the fact that it can often happen unconsciously, and we have very little control over it. Even more disconcerting is that this effect can occur at the cellular and biochemical level, predisposing our present and our future to formidable disruption. And since these conditioned responses can develop unconsciously, it's not a surprise that at times we feel out of control or unable to have any effect on our health and habits, much less our reactions to the world. Much of this conditioning, as I've discussed, operates at the limbic level.

Given the fact that conditioning lies at the heart of our habits, being able to recondition ourselves to react more favorably and healthfully to discomfort is essential. This will be a pivotal component in the retraining of your limbic brain.

Chapter 7

Externalization

The Dark Side of Creature Comforts

At this point in the book, you've gained an understanding of how discomfort plays a role in setting off your survival instinct, as well as how the cascade of biological events feeds the development of unhealthy habits. But a bigger question we have yet to answer is the following: What is actually causing us to experience greater levels of discomfort to begin with? And who—or what—is actually responsible for all this unhealthy conditioning? In this chapter, we will look at our triggers. In particular, we will examine how externalization is often the root cause of our demise, driving our discomfort levels to all-time highs. It's also the culprit in the ways we can become conditioned to live an unhealthy life.

If I had to sum up the definition of externalization and what it means for our inner survivalist, I'd say that it's the process by which we find ourselves increasingly affected by external influences and attributing more power and value to these outer reference points at the expense of our inner reference points. Inner reference points are simply our emotional and physical health, and our core beliefs. But with externalization, rather than our core driving our behavior and choices, we fall more and more at the mercy of outside influences and expectations. The end result is that we pursue goals and make choices that are incongruent with our true selves, and all the while our inner self is screaming a louder and more resounding No. And as agitance and discomfort levels are driven up by externalization, the threshold for setting off the survival instinct is driven down.

Just how do external forces working on our inner survivalist in everyday life create a more pesky, feisty, and overly sensitive survival instinct? To answer this question, let's take a look at some of our most common experiences that point to just how powerful the effects of our ever-changing world can be on us.

First, have you ever noticed that when you've gone back to watch an old movie that you enjoyed long ago, it seems slow and protracted? You can't get to the main point fast enough. Yet you recall that when you watched it before, it flowed better and moved at a good pace. Or have you ever reread some of your favorite books only to find them tediously slow and that it takes too long to get to the dramatic parts? Can you no longer handle long articles or blogs online, growing impatient and wishing the content were just whittled down to a series of quick bullets or a succinct summary of the topic? Maybe you're even wishing that now as you read this! So why does this happen?

Having taught for more than twenty-five years, I've noticed that I have to deliver my material differently today than I did earlier in my career. I now find craftier ways to engage my audience, and I use terse, pithy language to keep them listening. Early in my career, back when I learned how to create sound bites for TV segments, little did I know that this manner of speaking would become the communication norm in our society.

When did we become so impatient, with a need for things to be delivered faster? When did our attention spans shrink? And why do we find ourselves irritated, bored, or tuning out when things are not given to us in an expedient manner?

These changes may not seem all that significant, but they actually represent a much more startling change that is occurring at a biochemical level within us. And it is these biochemical changes that are directly and harshly affecting agitance and discomfort levels while sensitizing our survival instinct, transforming it into something it was never meant to be.

In the Beginning: Would You like Fries with That?

When did our need for "fast delivery"—with goods, services, and even written information—begin? Contrary to what you might think, it started decades before we had smartphones, laptops, and nifty gadgets at our fingertips. While this may sound bizarre, bear with me: I believe that the transformation of the survival instinct began with the invention of the microwave and the growing popularity of fast and processed food. If you can, take a moment to recall the days before the microwave and before the ubiquity of fast food. Do you remember waiting and feeling desperately hungry for dinner? Can you recall asking your mom or dad when the meal would be ready, only to learn that it would be done "soon" or "in an hour"? Maybe you remember feeling uncomfortable, but that you managed to ultimately wait until dinner was actually served. We learned that we could feel hungry and sit with our hunger and somehow survive it.

But with the invention of the microwave and the greater availability of fast food, we no longer had to sit with being hungry. We learned that hunger could be easily satisfied and quickly remedied. (A fascinating bit of trivia: In the 1970s, there were approximately eight thousand foods; today, thanks to innovations in food manufacturing, there are more than forty thousand foods available to us pretty much anywhere, anytime.) Although this was enormously convenient, it also made us less and less tolerant of feeling even mildly hungry. We suddenly developed a greater expectation for our needs to be expediently met when it came to satisfying our hunger. Case in point: Have you ever gone to an event or a friend's house for dinner and found yourself getting annoyed, frustrated, or even angry simply because the food wasn't served when you wanted it?

This is not a trivial point. What really has happened is that we've set in motion a growing fear of hunger if we're not immediately fulfilled. At the same time, we've made our impulses demand a speedier gratification. The end result? Just mild amounts of hunger can trigger agitance, discomfort, and a blistering response from our survival instinct. Our early ancestors might have gone days without food, but can you imagine that today? Most of us find it increasingly difficult to go a few hours feeling hungry.

More interesting still is the collection of symbols that have become associated with instant gratification, such as the brand images and icons linked to fast food chains, which can create discomfort. In the previous chapter we met researchers Chen-Bo Zhong and Sanford E. DeVoe, of the University of Toronto, a team that has studied relationships between fast food symbols, obesity, and decision making. You'll recall that when their subjects were exposed to the logos of fast food companies, it resulted in behavior that was more inpatient and impulsive. These researchers also noted a surprising link between these fast food symbols and people's ability to feel happiness. Not only did their studies' subjects select short-term goals over long-term goals, but they also found it more difficult to fully find joy. This kind of observation makes one thing very clear: The growing demand for instant gratification when it comes to food stretches far beyond the need to eat; it affects how we make decisions, increases our irritability, and compromises our ability to feel happiness. In essence, the need for instant gratification creates an escalating discomfort in the mind and body, and when this discomfort rises to the point where it's no longer manageable, it's far more likely to trigger a fear response and awaken our survival instinct.

We don't have to look too far to see the effects of this in our everyday life. I've noticed a profound increase in the number of patients who have a shrinking ability to manage frustration. They come in for help in dealing with what should be minor frustrations, but these frustrations are now capable of triggering a full-blown behavioral or emotional reaction. Take, for instance, the annoying experience of sitting in relentless traffic. More and more people are reacting in extreme ways to this petty frustration, from shouting expletives to engaging in "road rage" that can entail guns and violence—something that was extremely rare thirty years ago. Sadly, we now accept this as commonplace.

Recall James, from the second chapter, who began to rely on medications at the slightest sign of anxiety or pain. Although he reflects a much less extreme example relative to violent road rage, his experience is nonetheless similar: As his discomfort threshold shrank, he opened himself up to a raging survival instinct, which led him to exaggerated forms of coping that entailed a reliance on external means of containing it. Remember, too, the story of Kate, who was conditioned to eat at the tiniest hint of hunger or merely the anticipation of hunger. Like James, Kate exemplifies our growing inability to manage our discomfort, which affects our behaviors and emotions.

GOOGLING DISCOMFORT AND FINDING INSTANT GRATIFICATION

In addition to the proliferation of fast food over the past century, another, more recent trend has further helped feed our demand for instant gratification: the ever so powerful Internet search engines. A personal case in point: Not long ago I was taking a hike with a close friend and colleague in the Sierras outside Mammoth Lakes, in California. We were trying to recall a researcher who had published a specific study related to mind-body medicine. Both of us were acquainted with this man, but we couldn't recall his name. Almost instinctively we pulled out our smartphones and began Googling, only to find that neither one of us could receive a strong enough signal to access the Web. We both laughed and teased each other that somehow we were going to have to wrestle with the uncertainty and live with the discomfort until we completed our hike several hours later. We continued to make fun of one another as to who could handle the suspense better and who would break down with anxiety and stress. Although we had fun in this moment, the fact is Google's technology has dramatically changed how we live. No longer do we have to delay our desire for information and answers. We can get instant feedback and resolve any uncertainty in our lives fairly quickly. For those old enough to remember, in the pre-Internet era many of us would spend hours in the library running up and down stacks and perusing journals in search of answers and knowledge.

And, like the microwave and food industry, Internet search tools have influenced our ability to manage discomfort. On one level, they help us falsely manage discomfort by giving us a means to instantly gratify our needs and answer our questions, but on another level this is a double-edged sword. With access to such instant gratification, we reset our expectations across the broad spectrum of things we encounter in life. Suddenly, we want all of our impulses to be met right away, as quickly as the click of a button. Our growing discomfort then begins to be a more pervasive experience in our lives as it becomes increasingly impossible to gratify our impulses. As a result, we begin to experience a more widespread sense of discomfort in our lives, setting us up for a survival instinct that takes on a larger and larger role in our lives. In other words, while instant gratification has its short-term value in satisfying expectations, it ultimately leads us to expect short-term resolutions to all of our problems. And as many of us know, that doesn't always happen. Life is much more complex than that. If we come to expect rapid (and satisfying) solutions to our problems, then we're asking for trouble—we're positioning ourselves to experience much more discomfort when life doesn't work out that way.

Take, for example, my patient Zach, who was twenty-nine years old when he first came in for help managing work-related stress at his first job after law school. Like many young lawyers, he'd accepted a job at a large firm hoping to advance quickly and one day become a partner. But as is so often the case, young lawyers like him at prestigious firms end up doing quite a bit of the proverbial grunt work for the more senior attorneys. After a few years at the firm, Zach found it increasingly difficult to enjoy his work, because he wasn't moving up the ranks fast enough. He noticed he was becoming impatient and irritable, and having problems focusing, which prompted him to see me. In fact, Zach reflects many people of his generation that I treat—young, ambitious individuals who are easily irked and exasperated by the tedious process of corporate advancement. Many of this Y generation were raised with the philosophy that intent or effort should be rewarded above the end result. This ideology was meant to compensate for previous generations that weren't able to find value and appreciation in anything but complete success. As a result, Zach and his peers were praised routinely as they grew up, whether or not they totally succeeded. They are the "wonderful" generation, in which those who come in last place are awarded trophies and medals, and every project, work of art, and school paper is worthy of acclaim.

This unfortunately led Zach to feel satisfied with putting in less effort but expecting more in return—expecting to reap benefits for his efforts quickly. Thanks to his type of upbringing, Zach now had a difficult time dealing with conflict as an adult working in the real world. Avoiding it at all costs, he had a tendency to walk away from conflict even when it translated to serious consequences for him (and there was plenty of conflict in this firm, given the nature of the industry). All of this culminated in a very disappointed and discontented young lawyer desperate for relief. Simply put, Zach's need for instant gratification was combining with his falling threshold for discomfort, setting off his survival instinct.

THE NEW SEXUAL REVOLUTION AND THE ADDICTION LOOP

Zach's experience is but one of many examples that demonstrate the destructive powers of instant gratification, especially with regard to expectations. There are plenty of other examples, however, within the broader conversation about instant gratification that involve strong, sometimes undeniable impulses in the attempt to escape feelings of discomfort. And one huge category of these impulses, which I have treated in my practice, encompasses our sexual drives. At first glance, the need to be quickly gratified sexually may seem wildly different from the need to be rewarded immediately at work for a job well done. But these two scenarios have much more in common than you'd likely think.

There is no denying that all of us, whether we seek it out or not, have greater access to sexual stimuli, including pornography (thanks to the Internet) and sexual suggestiveness and references in the media. Ask any parents today what it's like to raise teenagers and they will lament how "different" the world is today, from a sexual-liberation standpoint, compared with the era in which they grew up. Even modern fashion trends of revealing and sensual clothing add to ubiquitous sexual stimuli. What this means for the limbic brain is a higher level of activity in its dopamine circuits, which then results in higher agitance levels.

In a certain number of individuals, this effect can crystallize into sex addiction, as they increasingly turn to sexual gratification as a means of managing their levels of discomfort. Over time, a lower tolerance for agitance and discomfort begins to develop, which leads them to turn to sex ever more frequently in order to get relief. Unfortunately, this type of addiction, particularly porn addiction, has a sharp downward spiral—as the addiction takes hold, only a narrower and more specific range of stimuli can effectively satisfy their needs. Sexual fetishes and obsessions, for instance, can become more and more specific, and those who find themselves developing sexual fetishes are less able to delay the gratification of these fetishes as their ability to tolerate discomfort rapidly shrinks.

My using sex addiction as an example is not as extreme as you might think. You may not have any interest in understanding this addiction, but the common denominator across a wide variety of behaviors that entail instant gratification is the same: The more that is available to us, the higher our levels of agitance and the more we need to seek relief. Our impulses don't lessen; rather, they actually intensify. It's the same thing that we see with alcoholics and drug abusers. In addition to the urge to feel the mind-altering rewards of drinking or using a drug, the more the substance is abused, the longer it takes to feel satisfied (hence the need to go back for more in order to quell the discomfort). So there's never an end to it. And as I discussed earlier, the more an individual pursues these addictions, whether it's food, alcohol, drugs, or sex, the more deficient that person's dopamine levels become, which further drives the addiction.

A most famous series of experiments studying this endless addiction loop has been conducted on rats. Researchers have examined rats given the choice of pressing a lever to stimulate the pleasure center part of their brain associated with sexual gratification or another lever for food and water. Needless to say, the rats die of starvation, barely able to pry themselves away from the stimulating lever, which has an incredibly powerful reward. And, as with human behavior, these researchers also note a lack of satiation in the rats, who take only brief breaks from pressing the lever.

Now I'm going to extend this observation one step further. A certain subset of people who use sex as a way to control agitance ultimately become more impulsive and are more likely to act on their impulses. This can lead to people reacting to their impulses in a much more grave manner, including pedophilia, engaging in violent sex acts such as sadomasochistic rituals, and participating in sex crimes over the Internet with minors. It doesn't help that we're exposed to widespread violence and sexual exploitation through television and film, which only feeds the cycle of agitance and discomfort.

But the take-home message from this rise of instant gratification in our culture is that it extends substantially beyond overeating, violence, and alcohol, drug, and sex addictions. It even goes beyond the satisfaction of our most basic or primary drives. We as a culture have become accustomed to immediate solutions to many of our desires and impulses. And rather than instant gratification reducing our inner imbalances, it only spikes them further, leaving our survival instinct to have an even more sensitive hair trigger.

The alarming surge in sex addiction, particularly with regard to Internet pornography, is why it's likely to be added soon to the addictions listed in the American Psychiatric Association's *Diagnostic and Statistical Manual of Mental Disorders*, otherwise known as the *DSM*. Sean, for instance, was thirty-two years old when he initially came in seeking help ending a serious reliance on Internet porn, which he used for sexual gratification up to five times a day. As you can imagine, this compulsive habit was becoming disruptive, interfering with both his work and social life. He couldn't get his work done and he began to alienate himself from friends and the woman he was dating. Although at first his use of Internet porn served as a form of pleasure, it morphed into an obsessive addiction that was serving the purpose of managing and containing greater and greater levels of discomfort, which is not unlike an alcoholic or drug user who reaches for a drink or a drug for the same purpose.

As Sean turned to pornography at the smallest indication of being uncomfortable, such as work demands and conflicts or problems in his relationship, he locked himself in a dangerous loop that fed on itself. Each time he received gratification, which was becoming short-lived, he further cemented his need for more. And the more he found relief with pornography, the more he found himself craving it. Ultimately, the treatment intervention that pried him loose from this addiction was to learn to manage being uncomfortable in his life and to no longer fear discomfort. This also had the effect of extinguishing his fixation on instant gratification.

Digital Demons

That day my friend and I couldn't access the Internet to answer a burning question while we hiked in the mountains was an excellent real-life example for me. There we were, far removed from civilization while tucked away in the Sierras, and yet we still found ourselves reaching for an instant solution. It's far too easy to fall victim to the magnetism of technology and the ease with which we can conduct research and business at the click of a button today.

But the growing computerization of our society is also strongly contributing to rising levels of agitance and our sensitivity to discomfort. We know from research studies that the act of using a computer creates a stressful impact on our physiology, resulting in increases in blood pressure and heartbeat and changes in breathing patterns. Computers are machines that rely on precise programming to operate, which is characteristic of compulsiveness and perfectionism—a style that exerts greater discomfort when certain demands are not met. This may sound bizarre, but it's not as big a stretch to see how the nature of computers can affect our perspective on the world. Think about it: Computers don't deal in the world of ambiguity, but rather in precision. Over time we can easily become accustomed to this absolute nature of the world. But of course the world is not nearly as black and white.

Another way to think of this is to consider what happens when you sit in front of a computer screen for hours every day. Eventually, you start to lose your ability to see outside this short range as your eyes remain focused on the nearby screen. In a similar way, computers affect how we experience the world, often putting us out of focus with reality. Which explains why the proliferation of computers in so many facets of our lives has led to a lower tolerance for ambiguity. We don't like uncertainty or situations that cannot be defined or solved in absolute terms. When you're dealing with a difficult person at work, for instance, you cannot just press the Delete button. If you're shouldering the weight of caring for a sick family member, you cannot just reboot that person and upload a totally healthy body. And should you find yourself in a car accident, you cannot press Rewind and take a different route. Life doesn't follow the rules of computer codes, nor can it be manipulated at the touch of a button like so many of our technologies can.

Our idealist, obsessive behaviors do not remain relegated to our computer work; they can be projected onto other aspects of our lives as well. Although compulsiveness and perfection are usually rewarded with high achievement, they do pose problems outside the work environment. As you can imagine, they can create significant stress in relationships, when our expectations remain so high that they collide with the inherently flawed nature of the human race and our partners—particularly when we look for our relationships to respond in such a logical and linear manner.

Of course, all of this is only exacerbated by trends in communication. The popularity of e-mail and texts, which command brevity, has transformed our conversations with others, reducing them to a very basic level. As more communication occurs in this manner, we begin to lose the ability to interact effectively in our personal relationships, for relationships require much more than sound bites and abbreviated sentences. And since we are already reeling from higher agitance levels, it's no wonder that conflicts can arise with much less provocation.

The Rise of Boredom and the Unrelenting Need for Stimulation

All of us know that the rise of computerization has led to a 24-7 lifestyle with very little opportunity to break away from the grid. Many of us feel like there's not enough downtime, or free time, to sit and do nothing or enjoy a few unscripted hours. Our lives can sometimes feel like we're moving from one text or e-mail to the next, constantly addressing demands at work and home—always "on." We are increasingly becoming a culture that is glued to our smartphones, constantly waiting for the next incoming message, while fueling our agitance levels and intolerance for discomfort. Recall that earlier in the book I described how Andrea's agitance levels were elevated in this manner, ultimately setting her up for a maladaptive pattern of avoidance. I also described how

Will became entrapped in a similar way, which led to a maladaptive pattern of insomnia. How often do we get edgy and restless when a long period of time goes by without receiving any type of message? And when you don't receive a message for a while, how do you begin to feel? Is it boredom, anxiety, loneliness, or even depression? It's funny how living without a text message or an e-mail can have such a profound effect on the mind and body. We can feel like we've been cut off from the world, alienated, or thrown into space without a tether. When was the last time you left home without your cell phone? And if you did forget your phone, did you feel unsettled inside?

We as a culture are becoming more dependent on external stimulation, and when we do not receive it, our agitance levels naturally begin to rise. I described earlier how old films that might have been enjoyable when initially viewed years ago seem tedious or slow when they are watched today. Film directors and editors have noticed the same trend, so to compensate for viewers' needs for greater stimulation and their propensity for boredom, they now create many more film cuts and transitions to sustain the viewers' interest.

We see this insatiable need for stimulation in a more exaggerated way among young people who take multitasking to the limit by doing homework, listening to music, watching TV, and returning their e-mails and text messages, all while having a snack. But this is not limited to the younger generation, for I've witnessed more and more adults picking up the habit. It's almost as if the increasing need to feel flooded with stimulation has gotten to the point that it's become an addiction, which makes us feel agitated when we don't receive it. And when individuals are asked to forfeit some of the stimulation, they actually seem to go into a state of withdrawal, which elevates agitance levels to the point of discomfort. Almost on a daily basis, I see this played out when I ask my patients to turn off their cell phones. For many, it seems painful—so much so that they attempt to quell their agitance and discomfort by silencing their phone instead.

Unfortunately, the need for external stimulation doesn't stop; instead it feeds on itself and demands even more stimulation, all the while fueling agitance to higher and higher levels. The more we engage in or are influenced by externalization, the lower our dopamine levels sink, and the more we become enslaved by our attempts to restore them. We in fact get trapped within cycles of unending agitance, discomfort, and a survival instinct that's always awake and alert. In other words, our inner survivalist becomes insatiable. It's similar to heroin addiction, in which initially the use of the drug creates a glorious high, but after several weeks of using it, it no longer generates as strong an effect. The addict needs increasingly more of the substance to replicate the original high. In short order, it becomes a fruitless endeavor, leaving the addict with growing levels of agitance and discomfort that cannot be discharged. This only fuels the addiction further as the addict desperately tries to quell his or her sinking discomfort threshold. And, like the addict, we as a culture are beginning to experience a lower discomfort threshold, which is leading to a large subset of the population being in a habitual state of discomfort and unhappiness—and a chronic activation of the survival instinct.

Other Sneaky Sources of Externalization

So far we've been exploring how more obvious external influences such as electronic devices and access to instant gratification are dramatically stoking our agitance and discomfort levels while lowering our thresholds for discomfort. But what about influences that are much more subtle, affecting us without our awareness? We can easily overlook the magnitude with which these undercurrents affect us. It's important, however, to note that the level of agitance and subsequent discomfort created are not strictly a function of how obvious, loud, or visible an influencing factor is. Rather, subtle and insidious influences can lead to a dramatic reduction of our discomfort threshold and undermining of the ways in which we learn to manage it.

We tend to think that watching TV, a movie, or advertisements is a passive event. But in actuality, serious amounts of conditioning are unfolding, and most of it we are unaware of. This is strikingly true with advertisers who are marketing their products to us using subliminal messaging and other conditioning strategies, which can entail both visual and auditory cues. You can expect that these advertisers and companies have spent millions of dollars figuring out how to deliver their message with the greatest impact. And they take full advantage of the power of conditioning to cement their message within us, often by appealing to our emotions.

The goal of such advertising is to make consumers take action. And the way to create action is to stimulate the consumer. That stimulator is agitance. In other words, consumers are made to feel unsettled if they don't resolve their discomfort, and the advertised product is portrayed as the solution. Obviously, advertisers are motivated by generating sales of their products. They have found that ads with the underlying theme that only their product can make you feel more comfortable—giving you more happiness, more energy, less pain, etc.—work. These ads also imply that without their product you'll be uncomfortable.

Another means by which externalization is boosting our agitance levels is through our growing connection with and reliance on films, news coverage, pictures, articles, and music that bombard us with an onslaught of carefully crafted messages and images. But the effect these messages have on us is anything but innocuous.

They in fact offer a powerful external reference point for how to live our lives (i.e., what to wear, what makes us happy, how much money we should make, what we should look like, whom we should marry or date, what is sexy, etc.). Further, they inadvertently strengthen our growing dependence on external references at the expense of our internal references, which may much more accurately reflect what is truly healthy and fulfilling for us. And the more externalized we become, the more discomfort we experience.

One of the most dramatic examples of how externalization leads to a harmful reference point is in the realm of body weight. As we know, there is a great emphasis on being thin in our culture. This is made particularly obvious in the proliferation of beauty magazines and dieting ideas, and the implied image of what's considered attractive in the media, especially on television and in film. Naturally we strive to achieve this goal of thinness, particularly young women. The obsession to comply with this imposed standard creates significant agitance for these women, which can then encourage extreme behaviors, such as obsessive dieting, purging, or excessive exercise. This places them in that habitual state of discomfort as they simultaneously seek to allay it. They become easy prey for fast solutions in the form of maladaptive habits that are traps in themselves, such as a reliance on medication or recreational drugs to deal with the discomfort. Or they can resort to stimulants to increase metabolism and weight loss while at the same time reeling from the side effects on their mood. In more extreme cases, someone might turn to cosmetic or bypass surgery in an attempt to permanently quell his or her discomfort.

But the hidden reality of our growing externalization is that there's often an inability to live up to this artificial ideal all the time, or at least in any healthy manner. The attempt to do so is made all the more frustrating by the fact the ideal can never be fully realized. So what follows is a blow to self-esteem combined with elevated agitance levels, which can eventually materialize into high levels of discomfort and the formation of maladaptive habits that aim to contain the discomfort and prevent the activation of the survival instinct. As I discussed in chapter 5, these solutions not only lead to a collapsing threshold for discomfort, but they also undermine our ability to self-soothe in healthy ways, as we come to place more emphasis on external solutions and have less faith in internal solutions.

Externalization can materialize in even more subtle ways. An enormous amount of research has been conducted to shed light on the biochemical effects of advertising. Neuromarketing is a new field of marketing that investigates our responses to marketing stimuli. Researchers use technologies such as functional magnetic resonance imaging (fMRI) to measure changes in activity in parts of the brain, electroencephalography (EEG) to measure activity in specific regions of the brain, and sensors to measure changes in our physiological state (heart rate, respiratory rate, and changes in the electrical properties of the skin in response to stress or anxiety) to learn why we make the decisions we do, and what part of the brain is telling us to do it. So advertisers that make use of this research are looking for very subtle ways to engineer agitance in consumers, in order to create demand for their product.

What if we have no conscious awareness of an external message? Can it affect us as well? Take, for instance, the last time you sat on the couch watching a television show with a friend or family member. The show cut to commercials, and you started to engage in a conversation with your companion until the show returned. Even though you weren't paying attention to the advertisements per se, did they still have an effect on you, however subtly? Turns out, yes. In 2007, University College London researchers discovered the first physiological evidence that subliminal images do alter the brain. In other words, our brains can log things that we're not even consciously aware of, yet which reach the retina of our eyes. This particular study used fMRI to prove that our brains can indeed respond to images our retina absorbs even though we're not fully aware we've seen them. This speaks to the subtle and insidious way in which external information and influences can affect us and influence our agitance levels and discomfort thresholds.

So like it or not, we as a culture are being influenced by factors that are obvious and others that are subtle, and sometimes subliminal. But these forces, whether conspicuous or not, are anything but trite and insignificant. Instead, they are having a profound impact in our lives, precipitating more externalization, prompting a devaluation of our internal reference points, deflating self-esteem, and disrupting personal and work relationships—all of which boost agitance levels while lowering our discomfort thresholds. This, in turn, provokes our survival instinct, giving rise to bad habits and driving our demand for consumer products. In most cases the effects of these influences have seeped in over a series of years to significantly alter our behavior and physical and brain chemistry, while fueling record agitance levels. Since these influences are unlikely to lessen, and are more likely to increase, it's never been more important to find ways to neutralize their impact.

And that's exactly where we're headed next. In the next part, I will discuss strategies that you can implement to minimize these influences on your agitance levels and begin to take control of your life and health.

Part 2

The Nature of Survival

Chapter 8

Managing Your Comfort Zone

Fifteen Simple Strategies to Stay Cool, Calm, and Collected

Much has been written in the past decade about the science of happiness. Scientists have found that we each have our own happiness "set point," the genetic and learned tendency to maintain a certain level of happiness, similar to a thermostat for your mental well-being. We can say the same is true of our discomfort set point—the genetic and learned tendency to tolerate a certain level of discomfort, before our survival instinct ignites and takes command. In the first part of the book I showed you how our discomfort set points have been lowered tremendously due to certain pressures inflicted by our modern society, resulting in our having an abysmally low tolerance for discomfort. It's that Cozy Paradox I described: In an age that affords us many comforts and opportunities to thrive, we've become hypersensitive to most forms of distress such that our bodies overreact to stimuli in ways that harm our health and, ultimately, our capacity to flourish. As you've also learned, stimuli can be any number of things, from fluorescent lighting that triggers migraines to calls from your boss that stir agitated feelings leading to sheer panic.

The good news is that we can adjust the settings of our inner thermostat. Angst and dread will always be part of our lives. But we can transform fear into safety, and build our "muscles" for dealing with uncertainty and instability. We can effectively turn down our susceptibility to the survival instinct, and make the instinct less reactive to the subtle and everyday hassles that are inevitable.

With this new understanding of how our survival instinct plays a tremendous role in our lives, we can arrive at better solutions to healing ourselves and staying as healthy as we can be. We can learn how to care for this inner part of us that refuses to be dismissed or neglected. By the time you finish reading, you'll learn how to successfully disengage your brain's reaction to discomfort when there is no actual danger, and develop new and healthy ways of managing it that don't involve unhealthy habits, overeating, pain, stress symptoms, unproductive relationships, or compromised work performance. You will even find that you can feel more comfort and safety when you are faced with difficult problems.

The pathway to raising your tolerance, however, starts with managing your agitance level, which you know by now has a dramatic impact on your everyday living and long-term health. And as you may also be able to guess at this point in the book, I'm not going to recommend the usual suspects for coping, such as medications or even talk therapy. You'll be surprised by just how easily and effortlessly you can lower your level of agitance—and the effect this will have on your discomfort threshold—by incorporating some simple and highly practical strategies into your daily life. I can't reiterate this enough: Agitance levels are different from individual stressors. Unlike stressors, which typically represent an external stimulus such as work demands, issues with a coworker or family member, or financial problems, agitance is free floating and is not typically experienced as a threat or felt as a moment of being uncomfortable. For the most part, agitance exists below our awareness, but it ultimately exerts a palpable effect once a certain volume has been reached.

The following are my fifteen proven ways to help you gain control of your agitance and learn to live in a totally new dimension. See if you can incorporate just one of these into your life today, and add as many as you can over the course of the next several weeks. Many of these require nothing more than conscious awareness and planning. They needn't take money, time, or unrealistic effort. I encourage you to read through all of these ideas first, and then choose which ones would be easiest for you. Do those first, then build upon that plan by adding more and more of these techniques, saving the most challenging ones for later. Once you know how to curate your agitance for the better, you'll then be prepared to work on making more room for discomfort, which will be the focus of the next chapter.

1. Take a Technology Time-out

In an earlier chapter, I discussed how technology is boosting our overall agitance. From e-mails to texting, surfing the Internet, and much more, our agitance is being pushed and maintained at unsustainable levels. Clearly, the role that technology plays in our lives is not going to diminish anytime soon. So it becomes more important than ever to find ways to better manage its impact on us. One way is to schedule technology time-outs, in which you take brief respites from your digital interactions, giving your mind and body a breather and a chance for your agitance to cool down.

For starters, I often recommend that individuals stop all technology involved with work at least one to two hours prior to bedtime. It is also valuable to limit technology when it's not needed. Often we are on the computer or smartphone far more than we actually need to be. As I also discussed earlier, we can become reliant on using these devices to fill idle time and deal with lack of structure. See if you can limit your "plugged-in" time throughout the day, and avoid cell phones, texts, computers, and so on when you really don't require them, especially when it comes to weekends, vacations, and evenings with the family. Allocate designated times when you're allowed to plug yourself in, but then be strict about the limitations you set. If you have children who are old enough to use technology on their own, set limits with them as well. It's never too early to teach good "tech hygiene."

2. Value and Tolerate Imperfection

I have also discussed how the rise in technology has resulted in a greater need for perfection, not only in ourselves, but in what we expect of others, which can be dangerous. Humans are flawed by design, and there really is little likelihood of long-term or sustained perfection in all that we do. The expectation of perfection in our relationships alone is significantly damaging, triggering arguments and conflict. Think of the last time you bickered with a loved one; it likely sprang from a place where someone's expectations were too high or idealistic.

Interestingly, however, the rise of perfection in certain areas of our lives, namely computers and electronics, has made some of us prefer imperfection in some cases. A great example of this relates to music. As music has become digitized, many musicians prefer the old distorted analog models of music—the human ear actually prefers it. Personally, I love early rock 'n' roll music, such as the Beatles' first recordings, in which the vocals are much more raw and the harmonies less perfect. I also enjoy music performed live more than the polished, recorded versions that are products of modern technology. And although the goal with technology is perfection, this may not really be what we should strive for outside our high-tech world. Working toward perfection is a recipe for unhappiness, resulting in a lack of acceptance and appreciation, and less tolerance of others. We never feel good enough or complete. So the real goal is not the achievement of perfection, but rather the journey of self-improvement—evolving, embracing imperfection, and gaining an ability to grow and learn from it. As one of my local colleagues and good friend Evan Shapiro, Ph.D., says, "There is no shame in missing the mark." Strive for consistency, but not for perfection.

See if you can find value and appreciation in imperfection; it offers us the opportunity for making constructive changes in our lives. When you find yourself demanding perfection, remind yourself that it's ultimately unachievable and that it's a setup for disappointment and unhappiness. You can find acceptance even when you're imperfect. Rather than basing self-esteem on external structure and behavior—such as proving x, getting y done before z, or winning a trophy—see if you can extinguish that frequent need to be perfect and to be acknowledged. Depend less on awards and accolades. See if you can do away with expecting perfection, recognition, and "trophies" in order to feel good about yourself. Rely less on external measures of success on which you base your self-value. Fuel your self-esteem from within, accepting that you cannot be—nor do you need to be—perfect all the time. I know, easier said than done. But consider this: You don't even need to be perfect at doing this exercise! Just put it to the test without any heavy lifting by spending five minutes on a routine basis, either daily or every two or three days, focusing on what you appreciate. I'll be covering the power of gratitude in the next chapter, but for now see if you can identify things in your life that make you grateful and pleased with your accomplishments without winning an award or receiving public recognition. Choose simple things, such as your family, your job, or the extra hour you had yesterday to sit and read a book. Research suggests that such regular practice of gratitude is correlated with improved physical health (e.g., better ability to manage stress and improved sleep) and healthier relationships. Also, learn to admire the peccadilloes in your partner and other loved ones, and to appreciate imperfect situations. The next time your spouse or partner, friend, coworker does something that doesn't live up to your expectations and really irks you to the core, take a moment to pause and remind yourself that you are accepting and testing out the challenge of living with imperfection. You can even turn that irritation into a source of admiration. After all, many of us were once amused by our loved ones' shortcomings!

3. Limit the Flood of Sensory Input

In part 1, I discussed how we often become reliant on being stimulated by multiple sensory channels—sounds, sights, tastes, smells, and behaviors. The effect of this is a constant craving, like an addiction, for more sensory stimulation. Without this flood of sensory information, it has become common for people to feel chronically bored and sluggish. This elevates agitance. A typical example of this is eating and watching TV while also entertaining company. Consider how many senses are being fed by this activity—hearing, sight, smell, touch, and taste, in addition to the physical process of talking.

To eliminate this perpetual need to juggle multiple sources of sensorial input, it's important to retrain ourselves to require much less stimulation. There is great value in learning to feel fulfilled and satisfied with little sensory input. Achieving this is much easier than you think, and it's not necessary to travel to a Tibetan monestary. Set aside certain times during the week for focusing on stimulating one or two sensory channels at the same time. For example, eat without any other distractions. Don't watch TV. Don't read. Don't speak with someone else, check e-mails, or read text messages. Activate just your senses of taste and smell. That's it. Or, for another example, simply read a book or newspaper without any other senses being tapped. An easy way to start is to concentrate on reading one article without stopping or multitasking.

4. Chill at Bedtime

Falling asleep at night doesn't mean that you're necessarily relaxed. Many people carry the stress of the day into their sleep, with the result that sleep is less restful and rejuvenating, or it's disrupted with wakeful periods, all of which can lead to physical symptoms in the morning, such as headaches, stomach discomfort, and a host of other symptoms. I have learned in my practice that having people listen to a relaxation CD prior to bedtime can make a dramatic difference in how well they sleep and how they feel the next day. In fact, if I had the opportunity to improve just one thing in my patients, then it would be, without a doubt, helping them learn to sleep more productively. And often the easiest way to do that is to change the nature of their bedtime routine. This is a particularly helpful approach for those individuals who find it difficult to relax before bedtime without resorting to sleep aids.

A CD (or any source of audio, including a portable listening device that can play audio files) at bedtime essentially does the work for you and involves no heavy lifting. If you have any interest in using an audio program at bedtime, feel free to check out my website, marcschoen.com, where you'll find my newest Stress Answer program. This audio program was used in one of my recent studies, which examined both subjective psychological and objective blood measures of resilience. By comparing these measures before and three months after the study, I found that using the audio program prior to bedtime significantly boosted subjects' physical and psychological resilience to stress while simultaneously lowering the inflammatory response in the body—all good things for health and sleep. The biochemical I looked at in particular was a cytokine called interleukin-6, which is highly influenced by the stress response in the body. In those who responded well to my audio program, interleukin-6 was dramatically reduced in the bloodstream. (The details of this study can be found on my website.)

In addition to testing out audio programs designed for bedtime, you can access an abundance of other sleep tips and studies at the National Sleep Foundation (sleepfoundation.org), and from there decide which materials will help you to enhance your quality of sleep.

A second suggestion I want to make related to bedtime is to go to bed sooner. A large number of individuals constantly delay the act of going to bed. When it's time, they begin looking for something else to do to avoid disengaging and letting go. If you are one of those people, test out getting to bed sooner several days a week, without having to make a lifelong commitment to do so. See if you notice a difference, not only in the quality of your sleep but also in how you feel the next day. Lack of sleep and lack of quality sleep have a direct impact on agitance levels.

For many, resisting sleep may have ancient roots related to the fear of letting go, wherein sleeping meant being vulnerable to danger, even death. Hence, avoiding sleep is a means to guard against this vulnerability. The problem with this condition is that over time you are teaching the body to resist sleep. In a sense you are teaching the body to resist its own instincts. And the more you get out of sync with these basic drives of the limbic brain, the greater the level of agitance.

For help in establishing a sleep-enhancing routine, you'll find a wealth of ideas in other books that focus solely on sleep, or go to marcschoen.com for a list of resources.

5. S-L-O-W Down

We all intuitively know from experience that there's value in slowing down. The problem is that this is hard to do, because our present culture tends to emphasize speed and multitasking. There is data to show that multitasking leads to more distractibility and poor concentration, very similar to the previously discussed results relating to fast food. When we're in speed mode, we have to be more on edge and alert, which naturally creates tension and agitance. There's value in slowing down, whether it's slowing down when we drive or just sit and eat a meal, speak with others, or run errands. We also would do well to place limits on the times during which we multitask. For instance, spend time with a friend without needing to be involved in other activities at the same time, such as checking and responding to texts and phone calls. It's remarkable how society has managed to accommodate these compulsions as acceptable behavior. Just a generation ago this would have been plain rude!

6. Stop Procrastinating

A fair number of people have a procrastinating style—a tendency to delay taking action or completing a task that should be done. In my clinical experience I find that procrastinators are often hardwired to put things off—as if it's part of their DNA and personality. I've also learned that these individuals need external demands and pressures to get things done, and often to produce their best work, whereas non-procrastinators can find it unbearable to wait until the last minute. So since procrastination may indeed be hardwired,

I'm not looking for people with this characteristic to make a 180-degree turn. Nor is it necessary to change dramatically for agitance levels to benefit.

As you can imagine, procrastinators typically create a significant amount of internal agitance. These individuals need to get riled up enough to accomplish a task, even though this has a compromising effect. The longer a person waits to pursue a task, the greater the level of agitance. The tendency to procrastinate rears its ugly head in the realm of decision making as well. Many of us today confront multiple issues at once that need some kind of decision, and typically it happens through e-mail. Rather than dealing with the situation or e-mail as it comes in, it's easy to delay it, resulting in a mountain of bigger problems that need to be managed and resolved all at the same time—creating a significant buildup of agitance that could have been avoided.

To counter this, consider setting aside certain days of the week during which you strive to procrastinate less or not at all. Remember, you're not committing to a long-term lack of procrastination, but rather certain times when you make a conscious effort to kick it to the curb. Just as you would set boundaries for your use of technology, set limits for your procrastination style. I realize that some people claim to thrive when they procrastinate—they say that they perform better once they are really pressed to take action and meet a deadline. These people may find it difficult to set limits on their procrastination.

For those individuals, I suggest that you identify tasks in which the stakes aren't so high and see if you can tackle those tasks sooner rather than later. For example, if you tend to delay managing your e-mails, aim to set aside thirty minutes a week to organize your in-box. Or if you're the type who is always fifteen minutes late to appointments or meetings, which causes you distress and ticks your agitance levels up, designate one day a week when you make it a goal to be on time. Pick a single routine appointment for which you're chronically late and aim to leave fifteen minutes earlier than usual. Don't feel you have to make a long-term commitment at first. Just test it out and see how it feels. Remember, the goal isn't to stop procrastination altogether. Unfortunately, that's unrealistic for the vast majority of procrastinators. The goal is simply to lessen the magnitude of your procrastination, which will automatically turn down the volume on your agitance. A little can go a long way here.

7. Stop Trying to Get It All Done

How often do we find ourselves getting aggravated by our inability to get all our work done and commitments met? We may even find ourselves saying, "If I just get this done, then I can relax, and feel okay about relaxing, leaving the office, or going on vacation." But by trying to get it all done, we can often get so worked up that we feel beat up and maybe even sick afterward.

When people are constantly trying to fit in more things than they can reliably and realistically complete in a day, agitance levels go up. Have you ever found yourself making multiple stops and running errands while also trying to get to an appointment on time (and finish a call on your cell phone *and* respond to a text)? Chances are you arrived late with some guilt brewing, while feeling a very stoked level of agitance.

The fact is, we seldom can get it all done. I have an expression for this: "If I actually ever get it all done, then chances are, I'm done!" The goal, ultimately, is to accept that in this time of explosive demands, paperwork, and deadlines, getting it all done is as unrealistic as striving for perfection, and our level of comfort and happiness should no longer be predicated on being perfect or getting it all done. Although it's important to strive to give everything our best effort, remember, there is no shame in missing the mark. And there is no shame in saying to yourself, "I've done the best that I can do. That's good enough!"

8. Embrace Uncertainty

Uncertainty is inevitable. It's human nature to find uncertainty very unsettling, and as such it's also human nature for it to create high levels of agitance within us. As we wrestle with uncertainty, we struggle to find ways to manage it—and many attempts can worsen its effects. When you look back at your past, can you identify a time when uncertainty resolved itself in a constructive manner? Most people generally find that it has, which makes uncertainty such a double-edged sword. Uncertainty can in fact be a friend—it can be a helpful catalyst to get things done and help you to confront unresolved issues. But it does fan the flames of agitance, leaving us with feelings of angst, dread, and worry. Now that we live in times of great uncertainty, it's best we find better ways to accept it, and develop an increased sense of comfort, tolerance, safety, and a genuine appreciation of it. Instead of fearing it, we need to embrace it.

As previously noted, in the next chapter we will review how to employ the power of gratitude in managing discomfort, which can have a profound effect on the limbic system. For now, when you do feel a sense of uncertainty, focus on a feeling of appreciation, and teach yourself to value it and achieve a level of comfort with it—despite how you might initially react to it. You can even focus on other areas of your life in which you feel thankful. With practice, this will ultimately recondition your response to uncertainty as you begin to view it in a more healthy and constructive way.

9. Kick the Anger Habit

Although anger can serve a survival purpose in terms of helping us to take action to defend and protect ourselves, in most modern cases, anger and hostility are overreactive responses from the limbic system that have no real utility. And they can pose serious health risks. It's well documented that hostility is strongly correlated with a higher level of mortality and age-related disease. It's even been linked to a physical deterioration of special chromosomal components called telomeres that have everything to do with aging.

Far too often anger becomes an addiction, and we may find ourselves angry going through life when there really is no reason to justify the emotion. Making matters worse is the fact that giving up anger is often difficult once it's become a chronic modus operandi, and there can be a resistance to doing so. We may falsely hold on to the belief that anger serves a purpose or even protects us, and perhaps punishes someone else. But in reality, it is only harming us.

In order to let go of anger, we have to go against the grain of the limbic brain's amygdala, overriding its nature to retain anger for some misdirected form of protection or even revenge. But anger stokes the fire of agitance, and only makes the inner flame burn stronger and with more heat. So consider giving up anger and embracing forgiveness, which is a significant predictor of mortality independent of other health and behavioral variables. Even if you find it difficult to fully relinquish all your anger, consider having anger-free days, in which you depend less or not at all on anger, focus on openness, tolerance, and acceptance, and even agree to smile when you don't feel like it. The field of dialectical behavioral therapy has found that just a half smile can be a constructive form of treatment. Participate in charitable acts that you might not typically perform, such as volunteering or helping someone else, which has been proven to help abate unrelenting anger in people. Consider finding other ways to deal with your hurt. This is also where traditional psychotherapy, hypnotherapy, and anger management groups can make a big difference.

10. Keep a Regular Schedule

A main focus of this book has been to encourage you to embrace discomfort in a more manageable way. In doing so, there are times when it's important to strive for some consistency and predictability—not merely as a way to avoid discomfort or fear, but rather to build up a stronger foundation on which to manage discomfort better. This is where establishing certain basic routines can be very helpful. In general, even though our outer mind or consciousness often likes novelty, and becomes bored with predictability, our inner minds or unconscious mind and body may seek predictability. Familiarity creates a powerful sense of comfort in the unconscious. Any parent with young children can see this in the repeated pleas to read the same book over and over or watch the same video repeatedly, even though to us it seems boring and repetitive. So it's important to strike a balance. By structuring parts of our lives to have this familiarity and regularity, we are fortifying our inner resources to successfully confront and manage discomfort in our lives.

Just how do you go about doing this? Easy: Start by aiming for a consistent bedtime routine and "lights out" time. You already know my thoughts about the value of restful sleep for agitance, so this practice has a double bonus. It also helps to establish regular routines around other activities in your daily life, such as when you eat and exercise. My goal here isn't to expound upon the benefits of exercise, sleep, or eating schedules per se. It's the consistency of these very basic aspects of our lives that counts. Keeping a regular schedule for all the things you do over and over again will by its very nature lower agitance levels. More important, such a practice will give you the resources to confront bigger challenges.

In fact, in *The End of Illness*, Dr. David Agus spends a great deal of time describing the benefits of keeping a regular schedule from a biological standpoint. He reiterates how the body loves predictability, describing how many of his patients mistakenly worry they have cancer when what they actually have is low energy and a poor sense of well-being. For them he prescribes a simple solution: keeping a regular schedule. That means paying attention to when you sleep, when you eat, when you exercise, and how you schedule downtime. Small changes in your schedule can have a profound effect on you physically. Look at how losing an hour of sleep or sleeping in a new location with different sensory stimuli can affect how you feel physically or emotionally. Even eating different kinds of food or eating at unusual times during the day can have an impact.

So clearly, small changes in schedule can influence how we feel and the agitance levels in our bodies. If the thought of sticking to a regular schedule in all that you do seems overwhelming because the nature of your life is erratic and unpredictable, then do as I suggested and at least start by going to bed and getting up at roughly the same time five to seven days a week. See if you notice a change in your agitance levels by creating some greater consistency. Then explore other aspects of your life in which you can create more regularity. Your body—and your agitance levels—will love it.

11. Expand Your Comfort Zone

Although it would seem that staying within your comfort zone would preserve your level of comfort, the fact is the less we challenge our comfort zone, the more our comfort zone begins to shrink—often without our awareness. Eventually, many more things begin to agitate us because of our diminishing comfort zone. It's best to think of the comfort zone as a muscle, and if a muscle is not worked and challenged, it ultimately atrophies and weakens. In order to prevent this from happening, we need to be on the lookout for and challenge our human tendency to want to reside in this old familiar place. We have no choice, really: **To truly experience and sustain some measurable level of comfort in our world, paradoxically we have to create some discomfort.** In other words, the experience of discomfort is the necessary precursor to the experience of comfort. But there are some things we can do that do not require heavy lifting or walking on hot coals that can challenge our comfort zone and help expand it at the same time. Here are some ideas.

- Consider driving a new route to work, or conversely a new route home.
- Try experimenting with a new type of food—one that has a very different taste and smell, even one that you haven't liked before.
- Try a new hobby or challenging endeavor. If you're not a dancer, then take a dance class. If you are uncomfortable speaking in front of others or are socially inhibited, then sign up for an improv or acting class.
- Listen to a new type of music, maybe one that you've avoided or disliked before, or something altogether different from your usual style.

- Read a book that challenges your belief system, one that you have some disagreement about or know very little about.

Right about now, you might be wondering if this conflicts with the idea of keeping a regular, predictable schedule in which you avoid "new" things, such as a new bedtime, a new lunch hour, or a new time for exercise. For clarity purposes, there's a difference between engaging in activities that expand your comfort zone and doing routine tasks that are part of everyday life and that relate to the core aspects of your survival (namely, eating, sleeping, and moving your body). By regulating these essential elements of livelihood, you are in fact creating a space for more sweeping changes in other areas of your life.

12. Take a Breather

It's so common to get into a certain work rhythm and find ourselves neglecting our inner sense of balance. Although we're getting things done on the outside to conform to or meet certain requirements or expectations, it's often at great expense to our inner rhythms. Put another way, how fast we try to get things done can often conflict with how fast our inner speed or rhythm wants to go to feel healthier or more at peace. And our inside rhythms can be so easily neglected and overlooked because they are less obvious and noticeable. To use an analogy, it may help to think of the ocean. For most people, they notice all the noise and activity on the surface of the ocean, while the water beneath the surface, which is much more quiet and still, goes unnoticed and is minimized and overlooked. Yet this water below is far more substantive and has a much greater volume than that which lies on the surface.

We are easily conditioned to the squeaky wheel syndrome—we

give our energy and attention to the immediate, while more primary and central needs, which aren't so obvious, get pushed down, delayed, or forgotten. Because of this, problems develop within us that we are often unaware of until they morph into something noticeable and demand our attention, eventually crescendoing into high levels of discomfort.

But there are some powerful techniques that can be practiced to better preserve the balance, and like the other exercises, they don't require a substantial time commitment. I've learned consistently in my practice that if patients take even one or two minutes twice or three times a day to reset their inner rhythm or frequency, their risk of experiencing symptoms is significantly reduced. I saw evidence of this in an informal study that I did at UCLA, in which we were looking at how hypnosis influenced the healing response. Subjects were given a small dose of the tetanus bacteria through the skin, which activated their body's inflammatory response. One group received training in self-hypnosis and were instructed to do their self-hypnosis in two-minute blocks, two to three times a day, while the control group did not receive the hypnosis intervention.

The hypnosis group healed substantially faster. We learned that the hypnosis worked by inhibiting the inflammatory response: Those individuals who took time each day to do a self-hypnotic exercise had a significant healing effect and a substantial reduction of inflammation in the area of the body that was being measured. What was particularly interesting about our findings was that the only area that showed this anti-inflammatory response was the one where the hypnotic effect was targeted, which in this case was the forearm. In other words, it was possible to target the hypnotic effect to a very specific part of the body. Another intriguing discovery made was the subjects' self-report after completing the self-hypnosis exercise: Many said that they barely detected a difference by doing it. Their outer, or conscious, mind was unable to fully identify and sense the huge effect the exercise was having on their biochemistry. This is an important point, because it reiterates the fact that our outer mind isn't typically capable of evaluating a process that is unfolding in our inner mind and our body. So whether the outer mind is aware of the change or not may actually be immaterial in terms of creating substantive results.

To get a positive result for yourself, it isn't necessary to learn self-hypnosis. You can achieve a remarkable effect by using what I call the Schoen Breath Technique originally described in *When Relaxation Is Hazardous to Your Health*. This step-by-step process is outlined in the following box. You can also go to marcschoen .com and download an audio file that takes you through it (use the word "breath" when asked for a download code). Try using this technique two to three times a day. It is best applied at your first awareness of your agitance level starting to spike. We'll also be using this technique in the next chapter, on reconditioning the brain to handle more discomfort.

Warning: At first, you might notice that the relaxation effect lasts for only a few minutes afterward and wonder how this can have an impact—very similar to the subjects in my study who were unable to detect the influence of the self-hypnosis intervention on their health. But remember, we are interested in the aggregate sum of agitance across the day. By punctuating the day several times with this technique, you ultimately lower your overall level of agitance. For example, if you typically run at sixty miles an hour and experience high levels of agitance and discomfort, by using this technique across the day, you may find that your average speed is reduced to forty miles an hour. And the more you use this technique, the greater the result, and the more likely you'll be able to recondition your body to run cooler, with less collateral damage across your day.

The Schoen Breath Technique

I developed the Schoen Breath Technique in 1984 as a tool for hospitalized patients who were in an acute state of stress. I had tried a number of other breathing and relaxation exercises throughout the years to relax these types of patients. But many times I found that it took too long for these exercises to take effect or that patients found them too cumbersome to continue on their own.

Determined to find another approach, I connected myself to a number of biofeedback monitors that could track my heart rate, blood pressure, galvanic skin response, frontalis muscle, and respiration levels. Over a number of trials, I was able to devise an easy technique that rapidly induces a state of relaxation and significantly lowers blood pressure and heart rate.

I have found that sometimes in as little as forty-five seconds, this technique can substantially shift an individual who is in an acute state of stress to a state of significant relaxation. I often called this technique my "95er," because it generally works ninety-five percent of the time. One of the reasons my breath technique can be so effective at managing agitance is that science has documented many times over the benefits of certain breathing styles on the brain and body. For instance, we know that breathing exercises directly affect areas of the brain stem that in turn strongly influence basic functions such as heart rate and sleep, not to mention breathing itself. Since the brain stem sends its impulses to the limbic system, we have the ability to adjust the limbic brain while at the same time influencing autonomic function to produce a relaxed feeling.

The following steps will take you through this technique.

First, sit comfortably with your feet on the ground and your back straight. Place your hands on your lap, with your palms either facing each other or facing upward. You can do this exercise with your eyes opened or closed. If you find yourself in a highly stressful and noisy environment, try to find a quiet space to do the exercise, such as another room, the restroom, or even your parked car (but of course, never do this while you are driving).

Step 1: The inhale

- Inhale through your nose while your mouth is closed. Take a slow, deep breath for three to five seconds.
- Inhale in a comfortable way. Do not inhale to such a degree that your chest feels overly expanded and tight. Do not elevate your shoulders or overemphasize diaphragmatic breathing.
- Place your attention on your chest or your head only.
- Imagine a sense of lightness, lifting, or floating in your body, as opposed to a heaviness.

Step 2: Holding the breath

- After completing your inhale, hold your breath comfortably for two to three seconds.

Step 3: The exhale

- For approximately a second, gently exhale a small amount of air through your lips—but not through your nose. Your exhale should make a soft "shh" sound (the sound we make when we want people to be quiet).
- Do not inhale. Wait one to two seconds, and make a second exhale for approximately a second.
- Do not inhale. Wait one to two seconds, and make a third exhale for about a second.
- After one or two seconds, begin the fourth exhale by slowly releasing the remaining air in your lungs, making an extended "shh" sound. However, do not deplete all the air in your lungs so that you end up gasping for your next breath.

- After several cycles, wait longer between exhales.
- Consider closing your eyes if you haven't already, and see if this improves the results.

Step 4: Repeat steps 1 through 3

- Do the exercise four to six times in a row. It will take approximately one to two minutes.

Step 5: Questions to ask yourself

- After completing this breath technique, do you feel a lower agitance level?
- Is your heart beating slower?
- Do you feel a pleasant lightness or calmness?

Remember, using the breath technique two to three times a day brings the best results. If you are under particularly high levels of agitance or stress, then use it more frequently. Typically, applying the technique in the earliest stages of agitance or discomfort will prove to be the most fruitful.

13. Delay Your Need for Gratification

In the previous chapter, I discussed how we as a culture have become accustomed to instant gratification, and as a result have developed a certain level of discomfort when we delay our gratification. Although I will discuss this more in the chapter devoted to upping your tolerance for discomfort, it's something that I'll highlight here. You may find it helpful to refer back to the Agitance Checklist in chapter 3 (page 44) and see how you fared in terms of your levels of agitance. Many of the questions correlate directly with your need for instant gratification.

Think about the areas of your life in which you frequently require instant gratification. For example, if you send an e-mail or a text, do you feel a level of agitance if you don't get a quick response? Or if you find yourself getting bored, do you need to quickly fill that space with something in order to feel more at ease? What happens when you get hungry? Do you feel the urge to quickly grab something to eat? Do you get easily irritated when you're in line at a store or the post office and the clerk is either new or taking his or her time? What if you feel an uncomfortable irritation or pain in the body—does it spoil your whole day? Are there certain people you find yourself more irritated or impatient with—people at work or family members?

You may come up with many other examples relevant to you. Identify at least two or three areas in your own life that drive your agitance levels up. Challenge yourself to hang out in these moments without having to take some form of action to mitigate your discomfort. For example, if you're hungry, wait a little bit longer than you would normally before eating something. If you find yourself irritated with a particular individual, practice being more patient and less agitated. Track your experience in a diary if you'd like, which is an excellent way to identify those areas you're going to work on, as well as make a record of your attempts to conquer your need for instant gratification. When are you most likely to succeed? When do your attempts fail? What methods do you find work for you to vanquish your emotional and perhaps physical responses when you cannot be instantly gratified?

14. Practice Hanging Out

We as a culture have become accustomed to relying on external structure, such as by being busy all the time and always engaged in some activity. But when that structure isn't there, it's easy to experience an unsettled feeling or agitance. The best example of this is something we see (and experience!) so often: When people are standing in line or have to wait, they pull out their smartphones in order to fill this empty space. As I also noted in the previous chapter, many kids today are being raised with constant structure, running from one activity to the next—soccer practice, piano lessons, a tutor, acting lessons, and so on. It's no surprise that this generation feels particularly challenged with open space that's not scheduled or filled to the brim. But as I've described in the previous chapter, constantly moving from one task to another and needing constant stimulation also creates higher levels of agitance. In order to begin eliminating this need, take time to just hang out, smell the roses, talk to a friend, or even sit quietly in silence and reflection. There is great value in doing so.

I remember, in my early hypnosis training, going to a place in the mountains and having to spend three days by myself with instructions to avoid speaking with others if at all possible and to avoid listening to music. I was there to write down my thoughts, practice hypnosis, and walk within a contained space. Since there were no cell phones then, there was no chance of talking to anyone on the phone or playing with a smartphone. I'll never forget that first day my adventure began. It was a Friday afternoon, and I was so uncomfortable that I couldn't wait to go to sleep to get away from my assignment. I was basically stuck with myself and my thoughts. When I awoke on Saturday I wished I'd slept longer, but there I was having to start the day the same way I'd finished the night before—bored and uncomfortable. The days stretched on and on and it seemed eternal. But sometime Saturday afternoon, an inner quiet set in and I was no longer uncomfortable being still in an open and unstructured place. And by the time Sunday arrived, I wished I didn't have to return to my regular life.

Try taking these time-outs for yourself. Expect that there will be an unsettled feeling, especially at first. It doesn't have to be three days, like my experience. Start with just an unstructured hour, then work your way up. Learn that you can ultimately find some level of comfort without having to immediately take action to settle your growing level of agitance. Keep in mind that at first, your new habit of hanging out will create some agitance, but with practice, you will find that you experience a greater level of comfort, and you will be able to stop being an "agitance junkie." I am hopeful that you'll find yourself making healthy choices, rather than choices that are ultimately for the express purpose of feeding the agitance junkie in you.

At this point you might be wondering what I mean by "just hanging out." This can take many forms. For some it may be sitting quietly and being still with no other distractions. But if you are accustomed to multitasking and engaging many senses at the same time, such as grabbing for your cell phone while standing in line, then try to limit doing more than one thing at a time. See if you can stand in line without occupying yourself with anything else, including nearby magazines or other distractions. Or if you're used to being with friends and texting or waiting for your phone to ring at the same time, try putting the phone away and fully committing to hanging out with your friends. Unlike the strategy I outlined earlier related to limiting the multisensory flood of information, in this exercise we are primarily interested in you learning to deal more comfortably with open space and less external structure and fewer distractions. See if you can endure moments focusing on a single thing, be it spending time with friends or just getting through a long line at the market.

15. Shake a Leg

It comes as no surprise that exercise can play a vital role in knocking down agitance. For our purposes, rather than attempting to achieve a cardiovascular effect, which might require longer bouts of exercise, aim for short bouts of exercise. I have learned that this can be enormously helpful in reducing agitance levels, and particularly in heading off the Let Down Effect. Examples of exercises you can do to gain the benefits of movement on agitance levels include taking a short brisk walk, jogging (even in place) for five minutes, going up and down several flights of stairs for several minutes, stretching, and participating in group classes such as yoga, indoor cycling, Pilates, kickboxing, and the latest craze, Zumba. Remember, it doesn't have to be a workout that will get you primed to run a marathon. You only need to move your body beyond its customary level of activity. And you can do this without breaking a sweat—even as little as five minutes several times a day can alter your levels of agitance. One of the ways I like to do this after a long day is to sit on the floor and stretch while I watch the news or even talk to good friends in person or on the phone.

Steering Clear

By incorporating as many of these fifteen strategies as you can into your life, which are instrumental in steering clear of the hazard zone of your discomfort, you can head off an encounter with your survival instinct. But what if you're already in the red zone and are looking for more direct relief? Well, in the next chapter, we'll examine how to manage your discomfort by boosting your tolerance for it using another set of strategies I have developed and successfully used over the years. What we're essentially doing is training the cerebral and limbic brains to react more productively to discomfort. These strategies help turn what would be a perilous reaction into a source of power.

It's important to keep in mind that the goal isn't to vanquish discomfort—this is unrealistic, and leads to a place of diminishing returns. Instead, the goal is to ultimately cope with discomfort in an effective manner, which can have a profound influence on your health and happiness, as well as how well you age. Remember, our reaction to discomfort can play a big role in biochemical alterations in the body, including the impact of your stress hormones, your body's inflammatory response, cellular aging, and even how your genes express themselves.

Chapter 9

Taking the "Dis" Out of Discomfort

The Hardy Survivalist

Life is destined to be in a state of constant change. I can't reiterate this point enough. And even things that bring us joy and comfort are doomed to change as well; one day they are available to us and another day they are not. We cannot avoid losing what makes us comfortable. So it's inevitable that we must come to terms with change and concomitant feelings of discomfort. Even that one word—*discomfort*—needs a new definition. We tend to treat discomfort as something bad and negative, something to avoid, dread, and fear. This is apt: We are wired to equate discomfort with fear and imminent danger because at one time that association served us well, helping us to avoid situations that were truly hazardous. But now, as I've been detailing, that's seldom the case. Our level of discomfort today is in most cases not externally created, like it was in early times. Although external stressors can influence our discomfort, more often than not it's generated by internal forces.

In chapter 5, I discussed how our fearful reactions and our inability to manage agitance leads to maladaptive habits, which are poor solutions. The purpose of these bad habits is to help us avoid pain, fear, or distress, and they trigger us to take certain courses of action that allow us to avoid confronting the uncomfortable feeling and fear. But they are temporary fixes, and they do nothing to improve our management of the discomfort and fear; they merely enable us to bury the fear—but at best it's a shallow grave, for the fear continues to smolder and grow, becoming a much more formidable force. At first this force can exist and even grow separate from our more conscious, cerebral brain. We can continue with our lives, feeling little impediment or impairment due to practicing these bad habits. But there's a price to pay, because what is actually happening within the brain is a so-called fractionation: The different parts of the brain—limbic and cerebral—are now functioning separately with their own agendas. This compromises our brainpower tremendously. And with different parts of the brain pursuing different agendas, it can be a little bit like Dr. Dolittle's pushmi-pullyu creature, and a certain level of paralysis begins to develop. I also discussed how these maladaptive habits, so often accompanied by diminishing dopamine levels, only enslave us further by squelching this critical brain chemical and ensuring that we remain tyrannized.

When this polarity in the brain takes hold, the limbic part that's being sequestered can, over time, metaphorically throw a temper tantrum, erupting in such a way that the cerebral brain loses full control. We already know that this has been found in post-traumatic stress disorder, in which the prefrontal cortex of the cerebral brain loses its ability to regulate the limbic brain. Technically this is referred to as dysregulation, which results in the limbic brain becoming overly sensitized to fear and danger while the cerebral brain has little ability to convince it otherwise. So initially, sequestering this limbic response may be similar to hacking off a reed that exists above the soil, while leaving its roots untouched beneath. The roots continue to flourish, strengthen, and expand underground while growing an even stronger foundation—eventually sprouting in multiple places above the soil in addition to the one where it initially appeared.

So we've really come to an important junction, where it's important to accept levels of discomfort in our lives. In Jack Kornfield's seminal writings, he talks about how pain is inevitable, but suffering is not. The goal, therefore, is to embrace discomfort in our lives, and to experience it in a more expansive manner. Rather than avoiding it, we can learn how to draw power from it. Just as pain can be an incredibly insightful teacher, the same is true of discomfort, making it something to embrace.

In many treatments today, the goal is to remove discomfort. I have already talked about how this has led to an explosion of prescriptions for painkillers. But it has also spawned many other interventions for dealing with it. The biological model has sought ways to use drugs and treatments to interfere with the registration of the pain response in the brain—to block the pain receptors. Most often this has involved medications, and in other cases surgical interventions that literally sever nerves so they cannot transmit the discomfort. Rehabilitation typically works on training the body to alter the physical causes of discomfort, such as retraining muscle groups or teaching the body to compensate for the pain by reacting in new ways. Traditional psychotherapy such as cognitive behavioral therapy looks to alter how beliefs and thought patterns influence uncomfortable reactions, with the assumption that by altering these beliefs and thoughts it becomes possible to turn down the volume or the cause of the discomfort. In mindful meditation, the goal is to learn to detach from the discomfort by accepting its presence while attaching less significance to it. This "top-down" approach relies on being able to teach the cerebral brain how to control the limbic brain. The term *top-down* comes from the fact that the cerebral brain, which sits on top of the limbic brain, is now exerting its influence from the outside in as opposed to the limbic brain exerting its influence from the inside out.

These approaches all have value, and many, such as mindful meditation and CBT, have been proven to make a notable difference, but each can also have certain limitations. I am going to introduce an entirely different strategy, one that has multiple benefits and can afford us the opportunity to engage both the cerebral and limbic parts together in order to gain a more comprehensive management and control over the discomfort in our lives. I call it the Survivalist Strategy of the 21st Century.

The Survivalist Strategy of the 21st Century

My approach doesn't attempt to assert control over discomfort by numbing the limbic brain with medications or by trying to lecture it via the cerebral brain. This approach encourages the limbic brain and the cerebral brain to participate equally, which will allow the discomfort to be managed more broadly, instead of in an absolute or unilateral manner. The more parts of the brain that we get involved, the more comprehensively and effectively we can experience and manage discomfort. So rather than teaching one of our brains to dominate the other in the top-down approach, we are invoking a horizontal approach that equally involves both of our brains.

Perhaps the easiest way to think about defining this strategy from a metaphorical standpoint is to consider a rainbow. But instead of a typical rainbow, which has a spectrum of colors, consider one that has only one color, and it's red. Clearly the red color would be our only experience of the rainbow. Let's say within the same rainbow other colors begin to materialize, such as blue, yellow, purple, or orange. Now our experience of red is changed. Rather than it being dominant, it now shares the stage with other colors. And in fact we may find that the color red takes up less space in the rainbow, and now exerts less influence, leading us to perceive and experience it differently as the other colors join it.

In a similar way, we are interested in bringing different areas of the brain to tackle what happens when discomfort is experienced. I call this building a *brain community.* And as other parts of the brain become involved, there is a *strength in numbers,* which dilutes the influence of the amygdala fear center. In other words, you can begin to experience discomfort less prominently. Like the color red in our rainbow, it begins to take up less space, while other sensations and experiences occupy a larger space. Now both the limbic brain and the cerebral brain's experience of discomfort has changed. In this way we are bringing in multiple parts of the brain to reexperience discomfort while forming a cohesiveness between them. It's important, however, to understand that just as the rainbow involves a number of colors, we are developing a *duality* (defined more extensively on page 168), whereby it's possible to experience discomfort even as we experience other sensations or feelings. Put simply, it's not necessary to banish discomfort in order to feel more comfortable. As you'll see, it's the presence of discomfort that in fact makes comfort more possible.

Said another way, you will learn how to retrain your limbic brain to interpret its experiences differently, broadening its ability to differentiate and react to uncomfortable situations. Rather than experiencing discomfort as a trigger for the survival instinct because it feels that we are in harm's way, we teach our instinct to respond with a sense of safety, heading off the tendency to react in fear. Meanwhile, we're teaching the cerebral brain that discomfort can be channeled in productive ways—such as to facilitate performance, decision making, and health. So now the limbic and cerebral brains don't have to resort to distraction or even maladaptive habits to manage discomfort.

Fascinating data shows how this neural retraining is possible. Recall that I described how the brain stem sends its primal impulses to the limbic brain, which then attaches meaning and significance to these impulses. In particular, when it attaches fear or danger to an impulse, it triggers the survival instinct, and then sends signals to the sympathetic nervous system to respond with a fight-or-flight reaction. The goal is to change the limbic and cerebral brains' reactions to the primary impulses registered in the mind and body. Scientific evidence now reveals that the amygdala, housed in the limbic brain, can in fact become better at determining fear situations. As an added bonus, we also can reduce the fractionation between the two brains, allowing them to integrate more so that all parts of the brain can work together in a coordinated and aligned manner. This type of coordination within the brain is a far more effective manner of using its internal resources to successfully cope with and manage our current world—a world that is not black and white and not defined in absolute terms such as safe and not safe. Our world is best defined by many different shades of gray, which makes it more appropriate that our brains become agile and adept at handling all these shades of gray using synchronized reactions and responses to complex situations.

Scientists have proven that the environment can influence the size of the amygdala. By "environment," I'm referring to social networks. Those individuals with more complex social networks have a larger amygdala, which helps them to better manage their social systems. In one particular study, researchers reported that the "amygdala expanded in conjunction with some other brain regions to which it is densely connected," such as the hippocampus.

So just as brain mass can strengthen with meditation, limbic structures, such as the amygdala, hypothalamus, and hippocampus, are also capable of adapting to changes that allow them to function in a less absolute manner. Capitalizing on this ability, we will begin by grooming the limbic and cerebral brains to differentiate better between the levels of discomfort, raising the bar before the survival instinct is pressed into action.

Getting into Total Shape

As you prepare to alter the fractionation in your brain, while grooming it for alignment, keep in mind that the long-term goal is much more than situational improvements in your ability to tolerate discomfort. Your ability to manage discomfort needs to become a permanent part of your internal fabric, which will allow you to tolerate higher levels of discomfort more consistently across the different contexts in which it arises in your life. You won't be "spot-treating" your discomfort in certain areas of your life as you would spot-treat a muscle in the gym using barbells—you'll instead be getting yourself in shape to handle any situation in which discomfort emerges.

The Creation of Alignment

To begin the process of retraining your brain's survival instinct, it's first important for you to identify one area of your life that creates some level of discomfort. Find something specific that creates discomfort but not to the extent that it generates a level of panic. For example, if you had to apply a 1-to-10 rating scale, with 10 representing the most uncomfortable ("I'm in a full-blown state of panic!"), then see if you can pinpoint an uncomfortable situation or experience that's closer to a 5 or 6 on the scale. It helps to compile a list in which you write down and rate different situations or experiences that are associated with discomfort (call it your Discomfort List). Once you gain confidence with using this method to retrain the limbic and cerebral brains, you can then tackle even higher levels of discomfort.

For the record, I want to be clear that this approach isn't meant to be used in lieu of professional help. For those with truly life- and health-threatening situations or behaviors, this should be used in tandem with professional help. Moreover, you should not discontinue any medication that you are currently prescribed. This approach is primarily meant to work in conjunction with any treatment you are receiving, and to help you rely continually less on those maladaptive habits you have developed to sidestep learning to manage discomfort better. Please remember to not do any of these retraining exercises while driving.

Remember, even as we tackle minor sources of discomfort, we lessen the likelihood that higher levels will materialize, while increasingly reducing our oversensitivity to discomfort over the long haul.

Let's consider some examples that could represent a level 5 or 6 on the discomfort scale. For the chronic weight loss struggler, it could be not eating for five or six hours. For claustrophobic people, it could be the anticipation of flying on a plane, driving on the freeway, or getting into an elevator. For others it could be the thought of public speaking. Or even the dread of having to confront a coworker or your boss, or deal with a thorny issue with your partner, parents, or children. Alternatively, it could be the mere anticipation of developing a physical symptom, such as insomnia or a headache. You could also consider those scenarios in which someone says certain things that are likely to incite your emotions.

In the following sections, I will be outlining a number of ways to begin retraining your limbic and cerebral responses to being uncomfortable. Feel free to test out each one of these different paradigms as a way to begin shifting your response to discomfort. Each approach involves creating different neuronal patterns within the brain and body so that discomfort now becomes associated with a broader and more comprehensive reaction of the two brains and body to discomfort.

Once you have selected your particular situation to use for the retraining, you're first going to master the Schoen Breath Technique, which I outlined in the previous chapter and which generally produces results in forty-five to sixty seconds. I'll be asking you to employ my breath technique at the beginning of all suggested strategies outlined in the following pages. But remember to check marcschoen.com for other ways to strengthen your results and build your *brain commounity.* Every time you practice this method, you'll want to do so until you feel some level of relaxation before adding another strategy. For example, if being fully relaxed is a 10, then strive for at least a level of 4, and of course more is better. The purpose of this step is to set the stage for reconditioning the discomfort experience with a greater level of comfort and safety. But a quintessential part of this exercise is to build your confidence in your ability to alter the physiology of your body. This is a critical point, and cannot be overstated. Developing this confidence is essential in learning to manage your discomfort more effectively. Although it isn't possible to have complete power over your physiology, it is possible to optimize what you can control. Feeling a greater sense of control is powerfully correlated with health and hardiness; thus it represents an important part of retraining your brain and body to manage discomfort more effectively.

Achieve Duality

Duality plays a major role in retraining our response to discomfort. For our purposes, duality refers to the ability to be aware of multiple levels of sensory experiences. For example, when you are at the beach, it's common to feel both a cool ocean breeze and the warmth of the sun or the texture of the sand. Or you may laugh even as you feel the irritation from a mosquito bite. To imagine these multiple sensory experiences is not a difficult task. But when someone is experiencing stress, anxiety, pain, or fear, it is not uncommon to view these experiences as absolute—that they are all-or-nothing events. For example, it's typical for those in pain to view themselves as either in pain or not in pain. Or, from a mood standpoint, you're either happy or not happy. Yet these types of emotions and sensations are rarely experienced in the mind and body in an absolute manner, even though they may be perceived as such. In other words, we can feel pain, but other parts of the body may feel completely comfortable or nothing at all. Viewing the world in absolutes sets us up for many ups and downs, whether it's significant pain or no pain, or happiness or despair. What's particularly troubling is that when we perceive our sensory reactions in this black-and-white manner, we experience our reactions in extreme ways. This explains why even a small trigger, such as a long line at the airport to get through security, can lead us to overreact at times with anger, sweating, anxiety, and even catastrophic thinking—all of which are hardly justified by the situation.

Learning how to experience the world in a non-absolute way—to experience it from the standpoint of duality—is key. Practically speaking, this would imply that it's possible to feel fear or discomfort while another part of us feels relaxed or unanxious at the same time. From our perspective, we are interested in learning how to feel a certain sensation or experience such as safety or inner peace even while another part of us might be concerned about an external outcome. For example, if you are feeling discomfort as you prepare to give an oral presentation to your supervisors, then the goal is to feel a profound sense of safety and peace while at the same time a piece of you still feels the discomfort. In this way, the amount of space occupied by the discomfort you feel is dwarfed by the space reserved for feeling safe and in control. The metaphor I like to use in describing this more precisely is to refer to the ocean, which has a surface filled with all sorts of turmoil—waves, swells, choppy water, and riptides. Yet at the same time the water just beneath the surface is calm and still, hardly affected by all the activity on the surface. In fact, the activity on the surface is just that—a mere surface disturbance. Similarly, what we're trying to do is develop an inner core that's like the water beneath the surface, in which all sorts of activity can transpire on the outside while we remain safe and at peace on the inside.

To achieve this, it becomes essential that we establish a duality in which two different events can in fact occur simultaneously. And notice that duality implies that these two levels can exist side by side—that it isn't necessary to somehow deny one for the sake of the other. This is exactly what we strive for in our lives: a state in which we can be busy and active, juggling a number of different demands, while feeling safe and in control in what I call the Inner Core State of Balance.

I first came to understand the importance of duality in a surprisingly fortuitous way. I had moved my office to a new location, but without realizing how being on a busy street (Wilshire Boulevard, in Beverly Hills) would affect the atmosphere inside. All day long I would hear car engines, horns, the slamming of breaks, and sirens. I was very irritated with myself to think that I'd chosen this location. I remember saying to myself, "Marc, what were you thinking renting this office when you do hypnosis all day long?" I then tried to figure out how I could induce a quiet, hypnotic state in my patients while the din of traffic and the constant interruptions rang from the street. To my surprise, I soon found that when patients learned to develop a trance state within earshot of all these external interruptions, they were far more equipped to establish these quiet states of being in their regular life in the outside world. I had never considered that doing hypnosis in a noiseless room while creating an inner peace state was not applicable to the world in which most of us live—with constant distractions and interruptions mostly beyond our control. I quickly learned how to make it possible for these patients to experience peace on the inside while still being aware of all the noise and distractions on the outside. It was through these clinical experiences that the concept of duality became a cornerstone of my work with people.

Another way of understanding duality is to see it as a means of creating a better balance between the outer world and our inner world, as well as between our cerebral and limbic brains. Just as you would anchor a boat in choppy waters knowing that it might sway and drift somewhat yet remain intact, you can create inner peace in a world of distractions, ultimately establishing duality. Creating this duality gives us a great opportunity to minimize the effect that the outside world and its distractions have on our inner core. By building this inner core, we in a sense gain much more control and safety from a constant state of distractions and interruptions, and the barrage of unexpected events in our lives.

APPLYING THE CONCEPT OF DUALITY

Since duality is a major part of retraining the brain to manage discomfort in a more productive way, we begin duality training by applying the Schoen Breath Technique to the discomfort experience that you selected. In this exercise, the goal is to experience multiple levels at the same time—to feel some level of discomfort while at the same time feeling a level of relaxation. This may seem counterintuitive, but the duality concept emphasizes the lack of absoluteness. By using this breath technique, it's possible to create a whole other layer of experience concomitant with the discomfort experience. Learning this duality and gaining confidence in your ability to experience it will be like building a muscle that you can use to shift your experience of discomfort in a much larger and more significant way.

Once you've practiced my breathing technique, the next step is to apply it when you're experiencing a mild level of discomfort in the situation you selected earlier. Remember, the goal isn't to be just relaxed and not feel discomfort. Rather, the goal is to have a sense of duality—the ability to feel discomfort in some parts of the brain and body while feeling even a ten percent level of relaxation in other areas. Of course, more than ten percent is even better. As you do this, notice which parts of the mind and body feel the discomfort or less relaxation. At the same time, notice which parts feel a level of relaxation. For example, maybe your shoulders and neck feel tense, but your chest, arms, and legs feel light. Pay particular attention to the fact that these two disparate sensations can coexist—that is, there isn't an absoluteness to your experience, but rather a duality. Now go back and redo the breath exercise, again inducing a level of relaxation. Focus on the same discomfort situation. What happens now? Is there a difference from the first time you did this? Is it possible to perhaps feel not only a greater level of relaxation with the discomfort, but a growing sense of safety?

The concept of safety with this duality is critical, for we are very interested in the ability to feel discomfort and safety at the same time. By learning that we can feel a level of discomfort and yet feel physically relaxed, we are in a sense teaching the mind and body that the body is safe even in the face of discomfort or danger.

Or to put it another way, the cerebral mind gains confidence in its ability to endure discomfort without having to rely on external means to manage it. At the same time, the limbic brain learns that discomfort is not a threat to the body's survival and can be experienced with much more safety. The importance of confidence cannot be overstated; it's natural to lack confidence in your ability to manage adversity, but by grooming the cerebral mind and sustaining a certain level of confidence in the face of discomfort, you can confront future discomfort with successful outcomes.

Label Your Discomfort

This strategy actually owes its success to the cerebral part of the brain. The technique was recently endorsed by Gerardo Ramirez and Sian Beilock, two researchers at the University of Chicago who reported on its benefits in the journal *Science* in January 2011. They've shown the positive effects of having students write down their worries prior to taking an exam. Doing so allows those students who have test-related discomfort to deal more effectively with it and to moderately improve performance. Their research confirms earlier studies, like those led by Dr. Matthew Lieberman at UCLA, that found that labeling fear responses can lessen the limbic brain's activity in the amygdala. In other words, when you identify and describe your discomfort, you lessen the fears associated with it. This may explain why keeping a journal by your bedside at night can be so effective in permitting more restful sleep. When you write out your deepest woes and concerns prior to bedtime, you in effect help tame your limbic brain and settle those nerves that would otherwise cause insomnia.

For our purposes, this strategy is a powerful tool in bringing the cerebral brain into much greater alignment with the limbic brain. We are not interested in using this technique to merely tame the limbic brain. Instead, we use this strategy to create powerful new associations between the experience of discomfort and alternative reactions in the brain. It's very similar to what I described in chapter 6 about pairing, in which two different experiences are associated to create a relationship between them. This strategy also builds on the concept of "that which is wired together, fires together," which I discussed in chapter 4. Clearly, labeling your discomfort builds on the concept of duality. In our case, it's the idea of discomfort and safety at the same time. The power of labeling cements this new association in a striking way in the cerebral brain, since the cerebral brain relies on logical thinking. So in a sense we are giving the cerebral brain tools to better understand the experience of discomfort. This strategy will be used in two chief ways. First, it will help to identify your areas of discomfort in explicit ways, such as by writing them down or keeping a journal. And second, we'll use labeling in the process of pairing discomfort with a number of other more positive experiences—a process you're about to learn.

Practice Gratitude

Gratitude isn't just about giving thanks or counting your blessings for good measure. As it turns out, there has been a significant amount of research that has looked at the value of gratitude in terms of discomfort and hardiness. Alex Wood, of the University of Manchester, in the United Kingdom, is one of many researchers who study the profound effects that a little bit of gratitude can have on one's quality of life and health. According to Wood and his colleagues, gratitude is "part of a wider life orientation towards noticing and appreciating the positive in the world. This life orientation should be distinct from other emotions such as optimism, hope, and trust." In a review article published in 2010, Wood and colleagues note that gratitude has a strong relationship to a number of very important aspects of functioning, including positive social relationships, more adaptable personality styles, and improved physical health, stress management, and sleep. Other studies have confirmed similar findings, showing that gratitude influences the experience of pain and overall life satisfaction and reduces body dissatisfaction.

So where does gratitude come from? What is particularly interesting is that it seems to emanate from the limbic areas of the brain. Recent research has shown that the "thoughtless" part of the limbic brain is actually where the experience of gratitude comes from. Because of this, we are particularly interested in drawing on the effects of gratitude and using them to influence the limbic brain's experience of discomfort. And by pairing these two experiences—discomfort and gratitude—we can begin to retrain the limbic brain's response to discomfort. As this happens, other parts of the brain—particularly the cerebral brain—become involved through the process of labeling, which again allows the discomfort to be experienced more broadly rather than in an absolute or unilateral manner. Stated differently, it now becomes possible to feel less threat and danger when faced with discomfort. **Remember, the more parts of the brain we can enlist to work together (*brain community*), the more effectively and comprehensively we can experience and manage discomfort. It's very important not to view this exercise as some form of new age therapy meant to whitewash reality;** rather, think of it as a way of building up other muscles in the brain so that when it experiences discomfort, it now has more strength and inner resources to manage it.

Just how can this gratitude-discomfort pairing be done? One of the most effective ways is to simply boost your sense of gratitude through a proven strategy: writing down and then thinking about certain areas or events in your life for which you feel grateful.

Following is a step-by-step exercise you can do to use gratitude in training your limbic and cerebral response:

Step 1: *Identify Sources of Gratitude.* Write down three to five events or experiences in which you feel a sense of gratitude. Examples include quality time with your children or partner, a trip to Italy, your mother's triumph over cancer, or the success of your business. If you cannot come up with the experience, then imagine one you would like to have and the feeling that would be associated with it. **Make sure that as you do this, you not only think of the experience, but more important, you focus on the feeling attached to it.** Lightness, warmth, openness, or other pleasurable feelings might be the sensations you experience as you focus on these gratitude moments. Once you are able to conjure up the feeling of gratitude, which is essential to this exercise, you are ready to proceed to step 2.

Step 2: *Perform the Schoen Breath Technique.* This will adequately elicit an elevated relaxation response.

Step 3: *Introduce the Source of Discomfort.* Now begin thinking of that discomfort situation that you selected earlier. Allow a certain level of discomfort to move through your body, starting with just a small amount at first. Next, go over one or two of the items that you selected on your gratitude list. Make sure to not only recall these items but to conjure up the feeling of gratitude related to them. Keep in mind that the goal of the exercise is not to vanquish discomfort, but rather to associate the discomfort with a feeling other than anxiety or danger.

Step 4: *Acknowledge the Duality.* We are calling on the concept of duality that I described earlier, in which it's possible to experience multiple sensory experiences at the same time. For example, you may notice that you can feel some emotional discomfort that registers as a tightness in your chest, while feeling a pleasant lightness or warmth related to your feelings of gratitude that you noticed in step 1. You are now enabling the limbic brain to experience discomfort in a broader and much less absolute way.

Step 5: *Bring in the Cerebral Brain—the Power of Labeling.* Now we bring in the labeling strategy for purposes of pairing discomfort with the feeling generated when you focus on feeling appreciative. You're using labeling to identify and acknowledge that discomfort and the feeling of gratitude can exist simultaneously. The labeling not only turns down the volume of the limbic response to discomfort, but more important, it seals the connection within the cerebral brain that a duality can exist: It's possible to feel discomfort and a positive experience as well—in this case, a sense of gratitude. Remember, we are not interested in extinguishing the limbic response. We're aiming to bring it more into alignment with the cerebral brain.

Once you can simultaneously experience discomfort and gratitude in the mind and body, use your cerebral brain to relabel discomfort as more comfortable and safe to feel. How can this be done in a practical way? Labeling does require some deliberate self-talk here, but for good reason. Use labeling to tell yourself that you can comfortably experience gratitude and discomfort at the same time. For example, if you have chosen hunger to be your discomfort experience, you would focus on being hungry while also tuning in to feelings of gratitude. In other words, you are allowing your cerebral brain to draw a conclusion that you can feel discomfort even while you're registering another feeling. This process also draws on what I described earlier about the importance of confidence, whereby the cerebral brain develops a greater confidence in being able to manage future discomfort in a more effective manner. The end result is that the cerebral brain learns to interpret future discomfort in a more productive and confident manner.

Step 6: *Repeat.* It's important to understand that creating change and reconditioning are not quickly established by doing an exercise like this just one time. It'll be important to repeat this regularly over time. For example, consider doing this exercise once a day maybe five days a week and see what you began to notice. Most likely you'll see that even in the face of dealing with the uncomfortable situation, the discomfort interferes less in your life—it's more tolerable and feels far less formidable, and obstacles don't get so much in the way of productive functioning.

Recruit the Power of Social Support and Trust

In our next exercise, we turn to the area of trust and social support. Social support and trust have long been found to have an intense effect on the limbic response of the brain. In particular, they are strongly linked to the release of the brain chemical oxytocin, which influences the amygdala and brain stem. Sometimes referred to as the bonding hormone or the love hormone, oxytocin makes people care for each other, promoting harmony, cooperation, and altruism. It also has been found to be a factor in allowing social support to promote resilience, as well as making stress levels more manageable. In other words, in addition to being linked with situations of warmth and love, it's also tied to stressful situations. When the going gets rough, it helps people feel more connected and less frightened.

Although the release of oxytocin is typically talked about in reference to women, men also produce this hormone and benefit equally from it, as it's involved in our fostering relationships, seeking comfort and consolation, and building trust and likeability. In one of the more provocative studies of late on this multitasking hormone, Hungarian scientists found that oxytocin also participates in the science of secret-telling—the mere exchange of secrets between two people can elevate oxytocin levels and help forge a stronger bond.

For years I've employed the power of group settings as a means of boosting my patients' success. In some settings it's about helping a group manage their individual stress levels, while in others it's facilitating weight loss. One of the strategies I use in these group settings is to evoke feelings of discomfort. With my weight loss groups, for example, I have my patients come to meetings hungry. I then pair this discomfort with the comfort of hypnosis, while drawing on the collective force of the entire group to provide social support. This creates a feeling of being bonded with others going through the experience as individuals work off one another in their emotions and generate strong feelings of support. Often I find that these treatments can produce results far superior to those achieved in a one-on-one setting. No doubt with this type of group treatment, it becomes possible then to associate the discomfort in the situation with the comfort provided by the oxytocin release, thereby sealing the association between discomfort and safety, which leads to discomfort becoming much more manageable.

Taking advantage of this technique is relatively simple. All you have to do is recruit a friend, partner, or family member to help you with the exercise. Begin by using the breath technique to achieve a level of relaxation. Next, you'll use the power of trust and disclosure to alter your experience of discomfort. Start by disclosing something uncomfortably personal or even something you've never revealed before (it could even be something from your discomfort list)—but do this by writing it down on a piece of paper and then giving it to your helper to read. Then ask him or her to do the same with you.

Now tune in to the feelings of vulnerability and discomfort related to having to share your secret with your helper. For many of us, vulnerability and trust stir up some level of discomfort, since these feelings have at times been attached to disappointment or being hurt. But in this exercise we are using this vulnerability and trust to elicit the oxytocin hormone to actually promote a level of comfort. By doing so, we are giving the limbic brain experience in associating discomfort with comfort and safety, which has been helped by the release of oxytocin. Follow this by bringing in the cerebral brain with the power of labeling, and relabel the discomfort experience as one that now leads to connection with others and the formation of strong bonds, inner strength, and a sense of control, comfort, and safety in the face of discomfort or adversity.

Draw on Empathy and Love

The next strategy draws on the powerful emotions of empathy, love, and compassion, which are strongly rooted in the limbic brain. Dr. George Stefano, director of the Neuroscience Research Institute at State University of New York College at Old Westbury, has written extensively on how love and compassion draw on the motivation and reward circuits in the limbic brain. His research, much of which has been co-authored with Dr. Tobias Esch of Germany's Coburg University, has added to a growing body of knowledge about what happens at a deeply biological level in the limbic brain when it comes to the emotions of love and empathy. His observations have been confirmed by several other researchers as well.

A striking example of how love influences discomfort and pain was conducted at UCLA by Sara Master, who found that pain induced in a laboratory setting was attenuated when the subjects were shown photographs of their loved ones. Interestingly, a study that was published online in late 2011 in the journal *Emotion* revealed how empathy has a direct impact on heart rate and a sense of calm or comfort, which is strongly influenced by the limbic brain. What's particularly interesting about this study is that researchers observed that empathy was more likely to be found in the less affluent study subjects, who were more physiologically attuned to suffering and quicker to express compassion than the more affluent. The researchers, led by Jennifer Stellar, a doctoral candidate in social psychology at the University of California, Berkeley, found individuals in the upper middle and upper classes were less able to detect and respond to the distress signals of others. The explanation? According to Stellar, as reported by Yasmin Anwar for UC Berkeley's News Center, "It's not that the upper classes are coldhearted . . . they may just not be as adept at recognizing the cues and signals of suffering because they haven't had to deal with as many obstacles in their lives. These latest results indicate that there's a culture of compassion and cooperation among lower-class individuals that may be born out of threats to their well-being." What makes Stellar's observations from the study particularly important is that empathy and compassion have strong survival value, and as a result become powerful tools that we can use to reset the limbic and cerebral brains' reactions to discomfort.

You might be wondering how Stellar's group measured levels of compassion among people. Unlike other areas of study, compassion seems like a difficult thing to evaluate. When Yasmin Anwar covered this story for UC Berkeley's online News Center ("Lower

Classes Quicker to Show Compassion in the Face of Suffering"), she brilliantly summarized how the study was conducted. In one of Stellar's experiments, sixty-four participants viewed two videos—an informational one on construction and the other an emotionally charged story about families coping with a child with cancer. As you can imagine, people were moved by watching the cancer video and reported feeling sad but didn't have such a response to the instructional video. But here's what else the researchers found: "members of the lower class reported higher levels of compassion and empathy, as distinct from sorrow . . . and showed greater decreases in heart rate as they watched the cancer family video." Anwar captured Stellar's conclusions in the following statement: "One might assume that watching someone suffering would cause stress and raise the heart rate," Stellar says. "But we have found that, during compassion, the heart rate lowers as if the body is calming itself to take care of another person." In essence, being compassionate had a calming effect on the body.

Since love, compassion, and empathy are very much at the core of the limbic system, they offer us another opportunity to create a tool for altering the limbic response to discomfort. This is made all the more effective because they involve the motivation and reward circuits of the limbic system, which entails the release of dopamine and endorphins. As you have already learned, the release of these substances is at the heart of addictive behavior and motivation. When behaviors become associated with these reward circuits, they become powerfully cemented and encoded within the brain. And by drawing on empathy, love, and compassion, we have an incredible opportunity to rewire our experience of discomfort.

A great example of this rewiring was once superbly demonstrated by Donald Dutton and Arthur Aron in their 1974 paper, which describes a series of experiments done with a fear-inducing suspension bridge. In this study, conducted on young males, the men crossed the bridge and were met by either a male or an attractive female. When the men were greeted by the attractive female, who asked them questions geared specifically to reflect their fear reactions (related to crossing the bridge), their experience of fear was tempered and altered by their sexual feelings toward the woman. The researchers concluded that once the fear was attributed by the men as sexual arousal (as opposed to the fear from crossing the bridge itself), the fear attached to the event dissipated. Yet those who were greeted by the man correctly attributed their fear reactions to their crossing the suspension bridge. This study is a wonderful example of how sexual impulses, including empathy, love, and compassion, influence the reward circuits of the brain, altering our experience of fear and discomfort. Although the study looked at sexual impulses in particular, these impulses emanate from the same place in the brain where we root our feelings of love, affection, and passion, which explains why these feelings become powerful change agents that we can use to alter the two brains' reactions to discomfort. We can now use them as tools to retrain the limbic and cerebral brains' reactions to discomfort by engaging the reward circuits of the limbic brain in a constructive manner.

In this exercise we will pair the discomfort situation or event you selected earlier with an event, memory, or person that evokes either love, compassion, or empathy. Remember, we are doing this to build your brain community, as opposed to whitewashing reality. For example, this could be the love you feel for your partner, your children, grandchildren, or even a pet. Or maybe you'll utilize the empathy or compassion you feel toward a certain cause as it relates to underprivileged people or those who have been victimized.

Like before, begin with my breath technique. Once a level of relaxation is achieved, focus on the situation that brings you discomfort. Once some level of discomfort is experienced, start focusing on what you selected to elicit love, empathy, or compassion. See what you notice. Do these feelings change your experience of discomfort? Do you notice that even though there may still be some discomfort, the nature of it has shifted—it feels less heavy, less piercing, or less distressing? Follow this by engaging the cerebral brain in relabeling this experience. For example, "I can feel safer and safer, or more and more comfortable even as I feel these feelings of discomfort."

Take the Challenge

Now we turn our attention to the power of challenge. The importance of challenge has been highlighted by social psychologist Salvatore Maddi, whose seminal work entailed following a number of telephone industry employees from the mid-1970s to 1987, while the industry was being downsized. Then at the University of Chicago, Maddi studied 450 Illinois Bell Telephone Company managers going through the changes related to industry deregulation. He and his colleagues did annual psychological and medical tests on the employees for six years before the breakup of the telephone company, and followed them for six years after. Maddi, who now is a professor at the University of California, Irvine, and is the founder and director of the Hardiness Institute, in Newport Beach, California, noted that two-thirds of the group fell apart, as they suffered from heart attacks, depression, anxiety, alcoholism, and divorce. The other third not only survived but actually thrived.

By looking back at the surveys done before the company's breakup, Maddi found that the successful study subjects shared three qualities now known in the field as the three C's of hardiness: a commitment to what they were doing, enthusiasm for challenge, and a sense of control over their lives. According to Maddi, these were people who struggled to have influence, rather than being passive, and kept learning from their experiences, whether positive or negative.

As Rachele Kanigan chronicled in her "Are you Resilient?" article for the *New England Financial Journal*, in a follow-up study Maddi and colleague Deborah Khoshaba found that the hardiest telephone company employees had similar childhood experiences, notably those marred by several stresses such as divorce, frequent moves, illness, or death in the family. However, these people had learned to view and react to this type of adversity with tenacity and a sense of opportunity. And it was this perspective that allowed these individuals to view their present predicament of adversity as yet another challenge. "They hunkered down at school, they worked hard, they found mentors," Maddi says.

The late Al Siebert, of Portland, Oregon's Resiliency Center, has also looked extensively into what he coined "the survivor personality." As reported by Kanigan, "In thirty years of research on Vietnam vets, Holocaust survivors, gunshot victims, parents who'd lost children, and others who had weathered significant trauma, he found that the most successful survivors tended to have curious, playful, adaptive personality traits. Other common attributes included persistence, optimism, flexibility, and self-confidence." It's no wonder that researchers in addition to Maddi have also found that people deemed more resilient or hardy don't get sick as often as other people and generally endure life's hardships and disappointments better.

Research like this has great application in our work, in which we are very interested in changing the experience of discomfort. Rather than allowing discomfort to evoke a destabilizing or paralyzing fear, which pushes the survival instinct button, we create a call to action and channel an uncomfortable situation in a productive way.

For this exercise, I would like you to select some type of problem-solving game or activity. It could involve a game of chess, Scrabble, or another board game like Rummikub. This game could be played with a friend or partner, or you could play online against a friend or someone you don't know. We want this to be a strategic game in which you feel challenged, as well as focused. Once you've selected the game, we'll associate it with your experience of discomfort to begin conditioning discomfort with strategy, challenge, fun, and focus. Start like before, with the breath technique, then elicit the discomfort experience, and then follow it with this challenging exercise. While you're waiting for your turn in the game, focus on your identified discomfort experience, and pair the discomfort with the experience of feeling challenged. For example, if you selected hunger as your discomfort experience, then focus on your hunger as you await your turn. Once this association begins to strengthen, make sure to bring in the cerebral brain by using labeling to cement the association between discomfort and feeling positively challenged, experiencing discomfort as an opportunity to be strategic and proactive.

Tap Your Inner Warrior/Gladiator

I call this exercise "finding your inner warrior or gladiator" because it's about using your inner warrior to recondition your experience of discomfort.

Begin the exercise by finding some kind of cue or imagery or a particular person that you would associate with a gladiator. It could be a scene from an old *Rocky* film, such as Rocky running up the steps in Philadelphia to get into shape; it could be a superhero, such as Spider-Man or Superman; it could be a particular athlete or Olympian. Or you might even be able to make this association with certain uplifting types of music (i.e. the theme song from

Rocky). Imagine that you're one of these characters. See if imagining yourself in this way or listening to the music does anything to lift your spirits. Then imagine yourself as a well-trained gladiator, prepared to take on any adversity or challenge.

As before, begin with the Schoen Breath Technique, then bring in your discomfort experience, such as feeling hungry, and finally imagine yourself as a well-trained gladiator welcoming adversity and only becoming stronger as you encounter more adversity. Imagine yourself breaking the chains that bind you and kicking away obstacles that stand in your path to your goal. Use the cerebral brain to label the experience as one in which the more adversity you experience, the more focused and determined you become. As in the previous segment, welcome all challenges that come your way.

Take Your Time

As you do these exercises, expect that they will need to be done a number of times to maximize the result. No doubt some of them will lead to stellar results, while others will be less powerful. Ideally, the more of these different exercises that you draw on, the better your ability to recondition your response to discomfort. As you become proficient with lower levels of discomfort, begin to take on higher levels.

It's important that you avoid tackling a trigger for extreme discomfort right off the bat, since it's likely to ignite the survival instinct and limit your potential results. Remember, the brain and body do not necessarily learn overnight. Although we all love instant gratification, substantive change does take time, and as with building up a muscle, repetition is rewarded. Be patient as you take on increasingly higher levels of discomfort, rather than going immediately from a low level to a high level. This would be akin to trying to get over your fear of swimming by jumping into the deep end; it would only lead to more trauma and a call to action from the survival instinct. Instead, you would start by getting a comfort level first in the shallow end of the pool, and then slowly saunter into deeper water. The same is true in learning to manage discomfort in new and healthy ways.

Let's take one more example before zooming our lens back out and heading to the next chapter.

When Tom came to see me, he was aspiring to be an Olympic sprinter. He had been successful through a series of Olympic qualifying trials, but then suddenly felt a sense of panic as he closed out the final stretch of the 400-meter sprint. It seemed to revolve around the notion of having to draw on all the reserves he had left and channel them into the final portion of the sprint. His panic led him to begin letting up at the point when he should have been firing up toward the finish line. To understand the situation more, I placed Tom into a state of hypnosis, and learned that as a child he would constantly see his mother choke on food and gasp for air. Naturally this frightened him and seemed to have made him unconsciously fearful of losing his breath. Now, many years later, as he headed toward the final quarter of a race (when he felt most out of breath but needed to push through it), this association between being out of breath and his mother gasping for air was causing him great discomfort and triggering his survival instinct.

It wasn't long before Tom felt out of breath in situations in which he didn't even exert himself. His fear symptoms during a race were spreading to other areas in his life. Obviously this was not logical, but as I've discussed, the limbic response, particularly the amygdala, is often anything but logical. In my work with Tom it became necessary to retrain his brain to associate being out of breath with something other than panic and fear. I began by having him imagine being out of breath as he ran on the racetrack while at the same time pairing this with his image of a gladiator, which in his case was the comic superhero the Flash, who was known for his brilliant speed. This began the process of associating being out of breath with being a superhero.

Next, I had him imagine running the race, feeling out of breath, then picturing himself as the Flash and leaving his mother increasingly in the distance the faster and farther he ran. This allowed him to create distance from his mother in relation to feeling out of breath. Finally, to stitch the association even further into his brain, I had him go up and down the stairwells of my office building to create the feeling of being out of breath and then paired this with relaxation, identifying with Flash, a sense of control, and safety. By the time treatment was complete, the discomfort of being out of breath had new associations—with safety, performance, and being able to excel to his potential.

What's Love Got to Do with It?

Before we move on to the final chapter, I want to take a moment to address an aspect to this whole conversation about discomfort that didn't belong in any other place in the book. Now that you've come to a point where you know how to cultivate a healthier comfort zone by taking the "dis" out of discomfort, it helps to understand how the power of this knowledge—and the skills you've acquired—can transform what is arguably the most precious and important facet of our human lives as highly social creatures: relationships, or the capacity to love.

Perhaps there is no greater place where we can feel discomfort in our lives than in relationships, for there is little else that can push our buttons emotionally. Many of us long for intimacy, and yet find it so difficult to achieve. And how ironic it is that the very thing we desire is so frequently the hardest to create. For most, the emotional discomfort related to rejection coupled with the fear of being hurt can become a powerful obstacle. This helps explain why moments of intimacy are often followed by periods of emotional distance, and at times conflict. It becomes nearly impossible to love freely until we have learned that it is safe to do so. And as I have learned in this journey, to truly experience the full depth of love, it becomes necessary to experience it from a place of being uncomfortable. In other words, tolerating discomfort becomes the ticket to feeling the vastness of love. And as long as we are unsafe with discomfort, true fulfilling love will feel like an unreachable shore.

The same is true of friendships. For rich friendships to develop, we must come to terms with our own ability to manage discomfort. A question to ask yourself: Can you really manage someone else's emotional pain if you haven't learned to manage your own? I think not. In my own practice I've experienced the clinical difference between feeling safe getting into the mud of my patients' discomfort and feeling unsafe with their discomfort and distancing myself from it. I learned some time ago that I couldn't help my patients unless I conveyed that I felt safe going to this dark place with them. If they perceived I was fearful of exploring the discomfort related to their painful issues, then it only validated their own fears of confronting and dealing with these issues. I had to master my fear of being uncomfortable before I could ever really be of service to my patients. And the same holds true for us to truly connect on deep and meaningful levels in friendships. If we are uncomfortable with being uncomfortable in our friendships, then our friendships will typically remain shallow and unfulfilling. All successful and fulfilling relationships, in fact—whether they are professional or personal—require that we manage our discomfort well.

There's also something to be said for discomfort inspiring us to reach out to others in general—to connect and seek comfort from our peers rather than continue wallowing alone in our own pain. As remarkably social animals, we owe much of our survival to the establishment of social structures, of communities and civilizations, and our capacity to build strong interdependencies. Studies that have looked at the role of compassion, for instance, have revealed that other people can perceive our discomfort and feel compassion. After all, compassion is by definition the ability to feel pity or concern for the suffering and misfortune of others. If we didn't have this quality, we might have been slower to evolve and develop as a society. Hence, discomfort can lead us to forge stronger friendships and social networks. Perhaps this is how empathy and love are capable of altering our experience of discomfort, making it more tolerable.

In this next chapter, we're going to look at the relationship between discomfort and performance across an array of commonplace settings we all face sometime in our lives. It offers a great "twenty-thousand-foot view" of this book's main theme, and will further equip you with strategies to apply to your life today.

Chapter 10

Survivalism at Work

Performance and the Art of Decision Making Under Pressure

Congratulations.

You've likely learned a great deal more about yourself since starting this book, and probably in ways that have surprised you. I hope that you've also become significantly more skilled in taking charge of the agitance in your life and living with much more discomfort, no matter where it comes from. There's a huge piece to my message in this book, however, that I've intentionally saved for last. It was necessary for me to guide you through all the previous chapters before getting to this one. Up to this point, I have focused on the role that the survival instinct plays in physical and mental health. Yet these instincts play a substantial part someplace else, and it has everything to do with survival and success. I am referring to an aspect of our lives in which every day our "survivalism" determines the results of our immediate and long-term efforts, for better or worse.

If I had to give one word to identify an area in which full-throttle discomfort—and its immortal and unyielding accomplice, the survival instinct—lurks stronger than ever, I'd have to say performance. When we have to work under pressure, it's vital to be able to make split-second decisions and react incisively. If we can't cope well in this situation, then our performance can be dramatically compromised. This is true for all kinds of situations in which there's a lot at stake: at your job, for example, where you may have to crunch numbers quickly, close a big deal, respond to lawsuits, or manage conflicts; during a test, from an admissions exam that will dictate your future to one for a potential employer; at an event where you're scheduled to speak to an audience or sell yourself and your services to potential clients; and with your loved ones, who depend on you to perform in whatever capacity is needed (as a parent, spouse, partner, etc.). If you are a professional performer of the arts, then you know the importance of nailing an audition. The sports world is also an area in which the dynamics of fear have been the heart of much research in recent years. And for good reason: More than ever before, it's not just innate talent or skill that separates the winners from the losers among elite athletes. Most of them have the same physical attributes and abilities. It's the capacity to manage discomfort and fear that separates them. So as we can see, our ability to manage discomfort and fear can play a critical role in performance—ultimately determining who succeeds and who falters.

Performance is much more than a one-time award that is stuck to a wall or refrigerator as it was in our youth. Now, more than ever, performance is a marathon, not a sprint. As adults we are left with much more important needs that are contingent on our performance ability. And you don't need to be professional athlete or CEO of a Fortune 500 company for performance-related issues to play a bigger role in your life and health than you ever imagined. Whether you're completing an urgent work project, scoring on timed exams, trying desperately to impress someone you just met, competing to beat your previous 10K time, or trying to outdo your partner's score on the golf course, your ability to manage discomfort and fear is key.

I'm a firm believer that one of the reasons we're seeing so many instances of the survival instinct gone awry in our culture is that few of us are actually trained in how to perform when faced with increasing demands. And therein lies the real problem: Workloads all around have gone up immensely in the past several decades. Ask any student or individual in the workforce if he or she has to do more in less time, and you'll hear a resounding yes. But when is the last time you were trained to convert your skills and knowledge into useful tools for situations in which you're asked to perform under pressure? There's no shortage of companies delivering services that promise to boost your performance or show you how to get more done in less time, but the vast majority of these programs don't teach people strategies for handling performance-related discomfort.

And for most of us, our first experience with performance under pressure began with school—math tests, oral reports, and so on. Yet, as a society, we unfortunately focus mostly on teaching people facts and information rather than how to perform well. I can't recall ever learning in school skills that would help me execute at test time all the knowledge I'd cemented into my head during my long hours of studying. Even programs geared to coach students through standard tests, like those to prepare high schoolers for the SAT or premed students for the MCAT, still concentrate on the knowledge and facts necessary for answering test questions. They fail to teach how to excel while under the pressure of a ticking clock, which may have nothing to do with the actual facts that are tested. They also fail to help students manage the competing demands of their discomfort levels, some of which are helpful and some of which are hurtful. As a result, most people are left to fend for themselves, essentially handing the reins over to their inner survivalist. This is why tools to help people manage their time better or practice "stress-free productivity" often miss the mark. Most of today's self-help books, for example, are rife with ideas on how to prioritize and break big goals down into smaller goals to fulfill, but no one is talking about the core issue here: being able to handle all those priorities calmly and safely by first and foremost managing the inherent discomfort. You have to work from a place of comfort before you can begin to do your best.

If you never learn to transform your discomfort into a source of power to perform optimally, then unhealthy levels of discomfort will inevitably take over, causing a serious obstruction to achievement. In fact, my work and others' show that discomfort levels account for poor performance in nearly sixty percent of individuals put to the test. It's sad to think that the mere experience of being evaluated can cause a majority of people to underperform rather than excel as they should. At the extreme, it's been shown that upwards of thirty percent of test takers in particular have experienced profound underperformance related to their personal levels of discomfort and its physical impact on them. What makes this important is that these early school experiences with test taking constitute the building blocks that influence our performance in later years.

As you know by now, once you become hypersensitive and overly reactive to performing under pressure, then every single demand placed on you, including the most trivial and unimportant, can spark fear. This is when those maladaptive habits start to develop and establish themselves, and as you also know, one of the worst outcomes of this chain of events is that it can lead your survival instinct to activate when there is no real reason. Suddenly, just your thoughts alone—simply *thinking* about being put to the test—trigger your survival instinct and related symptoms.

The Only Thing We Have to Fear . . .

. . . is fear itself. Franklin D. Roosevelt might not have known anything about the physiology of fear when he made this declaration during his inaugural speech back in 1933, but he was right to allude to the profound effects fear can have on us. As I've already described, our bodies go to war every day in trying to keep up with our needs, waging battles against threats that are not threats at all (and they surely aren't on a par with the kinds of threats FDR's generation faced).

In 2000, a most interesting study was published in the journal *Biological Psychiatry*. It was led by Charles A. Morgan III, of Yale University, whose team examined the effects of uncontrollable stress on the bodies of two distinct groups of people having to perform in extreme circumstances: Special Forces soldiers and non–Special Forces soldiers. Anyone familiar with the Special Forces, or Special Operations Forces, knows that this is an elite group of military men who are trained to perform dangerous missions that conventional units cannot. Special Forces soldiers need to be physically and mentally robust and have the confidence, courage, and skill to operate individually or in small teams, often in isolation and in a hostile environment. The recently exposed SEAL Team Six, which hunted down and killed Osama Bin Laden, is the navy's version of one such Special Forces unit. There's no question that, by virtue of their job, these people endure enormous amounts of psychological, physical, and environmental stress. And because of their uniquely extreme capabilities, they make for an interesting case study.

What the researchers wanted to find out was simply the answer to this question: How do certain biological markers of stress differ between Special Forces soldiers and non–Special Forces soldiers? The biomarker that they studied was neuropeptide Y (NPY), a neurotransmitter that is released by the limbic brain in reaction to stress. Research has found that this peptide increases with stress, and influences decision making and performance during stressful periods. High levels of NPY are correlated with post-traumatic stress disorder, while lower levels are correlated with resilience to stress. The researchers hypothesized that the Special Forces soldiers would have lower amounts of this peptide than would the regular infantry soldiers when exposed to stress. Surprisingly, the levels of NPY among the Special Forces soldiers were much higher than those of the regular armed forces. However, the Special Forces' NPY levels quickly subsided, while the regular armed forces' levels remained elevated. In other words, while the regular infantry forces become paralyzed by their discomfort and their survival instinct, the Special Forces were able to quickly manage their discomfort and their response to the survival instinct, and then channel their reactions in a productive and constructive manner. This explains why Special Forces respond so well in extremely trying situations. It's not that they don't feel fear and discomfort, but rather they have trained themselves to manage their discomfort and survival instinct much more effectively. As a result of this training, they are hardier and more resilient.

Christian Vaccaro, a sociologist at Florida State University, also explored this idea, leading a study with colleagues at Indiana University of Pennsylvania. Calling it "managing emotional manhood," Vaccaro and his team looked at mixed martial arts competitors, finding that these men have unique ways of managing fear that actually allow them to exhibit confidence. Those who lost their match generally attributed their poor performance to fear—not to a lack of skill.

Where am I going with this? Not many of us are going to train to become a Special Forces solider, but imagine having a mind and body that can more readily respond like one. It's possible—without all that hard-core military training. Each one of us can achieve considerably more success if we learn to manage our fear and discomfort in the many areas of our lives in which performance under pressure is necessary. Let's take a look now at how performance and decision making under pressure are influenced by the limbic and cerebral brains.

Decision Making Under Pressure

Earlier, when I discussed the seat of the survival instinct, I described how the survival instinct presses the HPA axis into action, whereby the hypothalamus of the limbic brain stimulates the pituitary and adrenal glands, activating the sympathetic nervous system. What makes this particularly important with respect to performance is the fact that chronic activation of the HPA axis results in the cerebral brain losing its ability to effectively work in tandem with the limbic brain. By virtue of its fear response, the limbic brain has now commandeered the ship and is reacting and making decisions based on fear, while drowning out the invaluable input of the rational, cerebral brain. The two brains are essentially working against each other. And like an airplane toiling to remain airborne with just one out of four propellers, performance becomes shaky and compromised. Rather than being able to reach its desired location, our metaphorical airplane is now looking to avoid crashing as it seeks a safe place to land as soon as possible. What's more, since the survival instinct's fear response drains the brain of the resources it needs to function at its absolute best, it cannot formulate and execute good decisions.

The idea that our tolerance for discomfort is tied to our ability to perform and make good decisions is not a trivial point. In fact, Nobel Prize–winning scientist Daniel Kahneman writes extensively on the psychology of decision making, and in his latest book,

Thinking, Fast and Slow, he describes the two competing systems that drive how we think: System 1 is fast, intuitive, and emotional; System 2 is slower, more deliberative, and more logical. Clearly, System 1 refers to the limbic brain and System 2 is the cerebral brain. He argues that the limbic brain is often not the best resource for making good decisions because it can be so flawed and irrational—even when pressure and fear are not present. But what happens when pressure and fear are involved?

In a fascinating study led by Antoine Bechara at the University of Iowa College of Medicine in 1997, researchers described how fear ramps up our aversion to loss. In other words, we are less likely to take chances when we feel fear, and we are more likely to see the potential for negative outcomes than positive ones. As a result, we will make choices that are based more on protection than on potential value. This is true even when there is no externally imposed pressure; in those cases, we are operating from an internal reference point of fear and discomfort that is independent of circumstances in the present. This has particular relevance to those individuals who are already carrying higher levels of agitance and discomfort.

Studies done by others have further demonstrated that we have an innate bias toward negativity. We process bad news quicker than good news, and we have a tendency to interpret situations in a negative way while overlooking favorable or positive elements. In those situations that are ambiguous or uncertain, the presence of fear leads us to interpret these situations in a negative manner, even though a positive outcome is equally likely.

Recall that in chapter 4 I described the heart of the survival instinct as a function of dopamine levels. As dopamine levels drop due to poorly managed discomfort and fear, we can become embroiled in an endless loop in which lower and lower levels of dopamine continue to fuel increasingly more discomfort. Then we form maladaptive habits that are meant to control the fear, which push dopamine levels down further. With respect to decision making, studies reveal that the suppressed dopamine activity directly affects the amygdala of the limbic brain, impairing its ability to "teach" the brain a lesson. In other words, the amygdala is essentially incapacitated by the abysmal dopamine levels and cannot tell the brain to stop the behavior that's causing the suppression. This explains why addicted individuals continue to make poor decisions and engage in their bad habits despite a constant barrage of punishing experiences related to their addiction. In terms of decision making, if discomfort is not managed effectively, individuals under pressure will continue to make poor decisions.

But what if we take the limbic brain out of the picture? When Peter Sokol-Hessner and Elizabeth Phelps, of New York University, collaborated with Caltech's Colin Camerer on this question, they discovered that if the amygdala is severed, our risk aversion is significantly impeded. Clearly, we're not going to sever the amygdala, which acts as the "first responding unit" of the limbic brain. But Sokol-Hessner and his team's data show that it is possible to change our distaste for fear. **Although negative thinking at one time had survival benefits, today we find ourselves saddled with this old negativity bias, which gets revved up even more so during uncomfortable situations. This explains why we are driven to avoid losses far more than we are driven to pursue gains. Or, said differently, we are wired to pursue safety above everything else.** As our illogical limbic brain seizes control, our decisions are increasingly shaped by quick judgments that undermine the cerebral brain's ability to make more accurate, calculating decisions during times of discomfort. All of this ties directly into performance. When we experience pressure-induced fear with respect to decision making, the limbic brain, or System 1, compels us to take protective action, bypassing the valuable input that the cerebral brain, or System 2, could contribute.

Let's first take a look at the various ways in which we could be asked to perform, and how our agitance and discomfort play a powerful role. You may not see yourself in all of these scenarios, but you'll certainly be able to relate to one or more of them. Then, I'll offer guidance on training yourself to perform optimally under pressure while keeping the survival instinct at bay. You'll be called to employ many of the methods and strategies described in this book, reinforcing all that you've learned.

Performance at Work: Hanging Out in the Discomfort Zone

Perhaps our work is the biggest part of our life in which we constantly confront making decisions under pressure. After all, our on-the-job performance can determine our career advancement, our salary, and our self-esteem. As a result, superbly managing discomfort in this environment couldn't be more essential. Many of the examples I've described in this book have in fact been about people trying to cope with work-related challenges. Recall my patient Zach, who struggled in his job at a big law firm, finding it difficult to stay the course in the face of discomfort. He epitomizes someone who needs to develop better skills for dealing with discomfort, especially for circumstances beyond one's control.

To get a broader perspective and understanding of the role that managing discomfort plays in the work environment, I sought out a successful high-stakes entrepreneur who has navigated the choppy waters of the business world for years. Robin Richards has a long history of triumphs as an entrepreneur and visionary strategist. He is probably best known for being the founding president and chief operating officer of MP3.com, which ignited the revolution of downloadable sound files and was eventually sold to Vivendi Universal. Today he is the chairman and CEO of Internships.com, the world's largest internship marketplace.

Robin's personal and work philosophy emerged from growing up in a blue-collar home where money was tight. The few times a year that he dined out with his family were painful reminders of how little they had, as he wasn't allowed to order certain things on the menu because they were too expensive. His mother couldn't buy dresses that she needed. From an early age, Robin was determined to make his life dramatically different, and to do everything possible to be the "master of [his] own universe," never being stuck in a job where he'd have to follow someone else's rules. This steadfast commitment has guided him very successfully in business and at home.

When I asked him about managing discomfort in his workplace, Robin lit up and emphatically expressed how it was one of the most salient factors in creating success. He had some interesting things to share. "Blasting through discomfort and being able to handle it is where success and the dollars are," he said. According to Robin, many people "can't take the heat," quickly becoming irrational and unraveling when the going gets tough. He feels that this often explains why so many business deals fall apart, as mounting pressure leads one to do or say something out of character. No doubt Robin is referring to what happens when people are reeling from their survival instinct.

Robin believes that anyone can succeed, but that it depends on who can tolerate discomfort and manage it effectively. Confidence for him comes not from success alone but from being able to withstand the discomfort. He feels that expecting to win is easy. But it's far more challenging and essential to anticipate discomfort and battles in business, which makes the inevitable hits hurt much less, allowing you to "go into the high seas with a greater sense of calmness." Robin lives by the motto "refusing to lose" as opposed to affirmations related to victory. He also believes that his ability to hang out in the discomfort zone gives him a competitive edge at a time when many young executives fear being uncomfortable and would rather avoid a conflict and discomfort at any cost. He thinks that a business leader gains respect from his adversaries and cohorts when they learn he isn't afraid of discomfort or conflict and can manage both effectively.

When I asked Robin how he navigates through his own uncomfortable moments, he said, "When a storm hits, I'm panged with anxiety, but it arouses my desire to do battle, and I work myself up in order to get tougher." As part of this mental preparation or "workup," he draws on his childhood determination to be the master of his universe. He embraces and welcomes the challenge.

This all sounds quite familiar, analogous to the findings in the study on the Special Forces who are often confronted with fearful situations in combat. It's not the lack of fear that creates a successful response; it's how the fear and discomfort are dealt with. For Robin, rather than avoiding discomfort, he welcomes it, seeing it as the ultimate path to success. Even though his initial experience with discomfort evokes a great sense of being unsettled—and no doubt a high level of agitance—Robin doesn't let it transition to a maladaptive reaction. Instead, he uses the discomfort as a trigger to take positive and constructive action.

But Robin also knows that as a leader, he needs to model and teach his employees how to manage their own discomfort. This isn't always an easy task, he reports, because so many young employees have grown up in a culture in which there is a sense of entitlement to being comfortable, successful, and happy all the time. Robin appreciates the old adage that says the fastest and shortest path to success is a long one, but this can be hard to teach the younger generations, who expect instant results and harbor a low tolerance for discomfort. He does what he can to psychologically prepare his people for difficult challenges by reinforcing the reality that things won't always be smooth sailing. In talks he gives in front of his employees, he reminds them that it's okay to feel stuck, to fight, to take on a battle or two, and to develop a reputation as someone who can handle it.

As with most successful leaders, Robin values the ability to build strong teams in his companies. He likes to create eclectic teams that encourage "cross-pollination"—a combination of different personality types, work ethics, and even discomfort thresholds. Of course, this often generates debates and disagreements, but he finds these teams to be more successful than homogeneous ones. And when dissonance inevitably develops, he encourages them to persevere, and to perceive the discomfort as an important ingredient for success. He also offers himself as a template, showing his employees how he leverages discomfort to spark productivity. Just by admitting his own challenges and educating them on the fact that discomfort is an essential ingredient of success, he can strengthen his teams' performance and resolve. And, as with Special Forces training, he grooms his employees to transform discomfort into successful action.

Aside from being tested in our roles at work, we all face other, more traditional tests in our lives, which start very early on in our youth—setting us up with the knowledge of how to deal with every type of "test" thereafter, be it work related or in the relationships we keep.

Academic and Test Performance: Working Under the Gun

Unlike older generations, who probably didn't experience their first encounter with an out-of-control survival instinct until they reached adulthood, or at least until their teenage years, nowadays kids vying for coveted spots at schools are having to wrestle with their survival instinct more frequently and at an increasingly younger age. And, as you can imagine, they are ill equipped in many cases to deal with this in healthy ways. As they struggle with coping, they often fail to notice that this silent battle seeps into other areas of their lives, changing how they behave, socialize, and make decisions until it becomes nearly impossible to overlook.

Take, for example, my patient Jenna, a bright and promising young woman whose excellence in school began to take a serious turn when her levels of agitance exceeded her discomfort threshold and she could no longer perform on her school exams. Jenna was about to begin the eleventh grade when she first came to see me. At the time, test taking had developed into a big obstacle in her life; she experienced panic and anxiety, which necessitated her reliance on medications to manage. It didn't help that she was entering a grade when the ability to excel at taking tests would become increasingly pivotal to her future success, especially with the SAT and college applications on the horizon. For Jenna, symptoms were fueled by a fear of failure. They started days before exams, as she would find herself with an upset stomach, nausea, and insomnia, even vomiting the day of an exam. During a test, she'd lose focus easily, suffer stomach pains and memory loss, and essentially panic as if her life depended on her performance.

Jenna wasn't an average student. Much to the contrary, she was a straight-A student enrolled in a number of Advanced Placement courses. Suffice it to say she was a seasoned test taker who had done well during her school years and had high expectations of herself. But over time, her test-related symptoms, negative thought patterns around exams, and particularly her fear of failure began to soar. By the eleventh grade, her anxiety had progressed to the point that it was now part of the test-taking process. In other words, her symptomatic reactions materialized whether they were merited or not—whether the exam was difficult or not. This is what I call test habits.

Like so many of her classmates, Jenna was a victim of externalization. She engaged in many agitance-raising activities, such as watching television, snacking, texting, and studying all at the same time. Her swelling agitance was exacerbated by the fact that she'd work at the computer or on homework all the way up until bedtime. In the past, Jenna's agitance levels had been under reasonable control, but at the onset of eleventh grade (feared by all college-bound students), they began to peak. Eventually, her high agitance combined with her school stressors, and, like a chemical reaction, her discomfort levels soared enough to ignite her survival instinct, culminating in significantly more frequent symptomatic episodes. Her mood was also changing. Her mother described Jenna as being short, uptight, irritable, angry, and feeling burdened. When I asked Jenna about being so worked up about her exams, she said that she was accustomed to feeling that she needed to be ramped up and upset in order to succeed. This reaction was Jenna's test habit. But now she realized that being ramped up was taking control of her life and ruining her ability to succeed. It was time to make a change.

I bring up Jenna's story because it's so symbolic of how many of us react to the rigors of having to perform in an extreme setting, which in her case was formal test taking. Some of us experience our first test when we "apply" for kindergarten, and from there we encounter routine testing throughout our lives in both academic and nonacademic settings. We can face testing in our professional lives, or as candidates for jobs at companies that want to test our personality, among many other attributes and skills. Often the experience of facing a test entails a serious double whammy: an underground stream of fear or tension springing from our history of taking exams and from the present trepidation related to not knowing how our performance will affect our future.

Jenna, by the way, overcame her problems with test taking and learned to thrive both at school and in her personal life. I began by helping her first lower her agitance levels in general. This entailed modifying her need for constant stimulation and her reliance on external solutions, including the antianxiety medication (Buspar) that she'd come to depend upon to feel an inner sense of calm. My goal for her was to help her approach her studying and test taking from a place of lower agitance, while reducing the factors that were feeding it. It then became possible for her to associate her schoolwork with an entirely different inner atmosphere and to achieve a balance between the limbic and cerebral brains.

She also worked on the act of test taking by practicing answering test questions in a more balanced brain state, while learning to experience discomfort as a performance enhancer. Since it's pointless and unconstructive to fully eliminate negative thoughts, which will always be there to some degree, it makes far more sense to accept their presence and strip away or neutralize their power. (Besides, anything we try to push away or ignore only becomes stronger.) As I lowered Jenna's unmanageable levels of discomfort and altered the power of her negative thinking, I helped her to use a healthy dose of discomfort to improve her performance, which ultimately encouraged her survival instinct to retreat so that it was totally out of the picture in her test taking. By doing so, I built a new set of effective test habits for Jenna so that discomfort and negative thoughts related to test taking and studying were now associated with test performance—a conditioning that made test taking success-driven rather than fear-driven. Put simply, it was no longer a success-threatening obstacle in her life.

Survival of the "Fittest": Sports Performance

Our experience with tests in those early days of our academic life can set the tone for how we perform for the rest of our lives; the same is true for people who play sports as kids. Those experiences on playgrounds, soccer fields, and basketball courts can have lifelong effects on one's ability to perform. And as with academic performance, the importance of sports performance in our culture has spiraled upward both in the world of professional sports and in smaller arenas—all the way down to the Little Leaguer in elementary school. In fact, one of my earliest memories related to performance under pressure is of standing on the pitching mound at nine years old, with all eyes on me—those of my fellow players, the opposing players, and people in the stands waiting to see my next pitch. Of course, I was hoping that somehow I would not hit the batter and that I would find a way to get the ball over the plate, which was not altogether different from my performance anxiety related to treating Mikael's hiccups decades later. This type of performance-related discomfort begins early, and it doesn't stop. If you are like most people, it can continue to haunt you.

We see performance-related discomfort in the sports world every day. Just turn on the TV and admire those players who instinctively react well, versus those who crack under pressure and make poor decisions. Consider the tennis player who defensively hits lobs and keeps his opponent in the game instead of going for a slam to win the point. Consider the professional basketball player who can nail ninety percent of his free throws in practice, but turns to mush during the game and sinks only a miserable fifty percent. Perhaps one of the most remarkable attributes that makes elite athletes in the class of Kobe Bryant and Peyton Manning so great is the fact that they thrive in extremely uncomfortable situations.

Earlier in this chapter I referred to Vaccaro's study on mixed martial artists, in which the fighters attributed their losses to their inability to manage fear. And with the increased emphasis on sports performance, fear in sports is at an all-time high. But this fear can show up in hidden ways. Take, for example, my patient Martin. When he came to see me he was a college basketball star with aspirations of playing in the NBA. Although never a stellar free throw shooter, during his senior year, when he was being considered by pro scouts, he noticed that his ability to make the hoops had seriously deteriorated, shrinking from seventy percent to thirty-five percent. His off-the-court practice made little difference, and it wasn't long before his shooting form became stiff and awkward; rather than shooting the ball, he was now pushing the ball to the hoop. What made things worse was the fact that his teammates and coaches were on his back to improve, while the fans had little patience, routinely moaning and ridiculing him when he came to the line to shoot. The prospect of standing on the free throw line with every eye in the arena on him became enormously uncomfortable, spiking dread and fear. The survival instinct eventually took hold, which eroded his confidence and began to seriously undermine even his non–free throw shooting.

After questioning Martin, I learned that his escalating fear in terms of performance was not actually anything new—it had begun years before, in elementary school. Martin was an average to above-average student back then, and what unhinged him the most were the times he had to give an oral report. He could vividly recall the sensation of being paralyzed with fear. He could hardly speak. His classmates made fun of him while his teacher showed signs of being exasperated. Soon enough, just the prospect of giving an oral report led to substantial fear. So when his name was called to stand up, he could see his classmates shifting in their chairs, moaning, and laughing. Now, years later, when the pressure was on him to perform in his senior year, he was freezing again and detecting a similar level of frustration and humiliation in his teammates, coaches, and fans. The experience was a carbon copy of his earlier school days. As he stood on the line to make free throws, it was as if he was back in school giving an oral report, crippled by fear and unable to perform.

Whether you're a pro or not, some level of discomfort is to be expected at the free throw line during game time. It's normal. For Martin, the goal wasn't to banish the discomfort he felt at the line, but instead to manage it more effectively. By learning that his present fear had its roots in his childhood experiences in school, I was able to help Martin separate his performance-related discomfort in basketball from those past fears that were no longer relevant. And he quickly got his game back on.

You're On!

Similar to the sports world, anyone who has to respond to the metaphorical gun going off in more everyday experiences—from having to be poised for a work-related function to juggling competing demands at home—knows that the pressure can quickly mount. In my practice, I see a lot of patients in the entertainment industry who are well acquainted with the audition experience. They know all too well that their ability to perform at their absolute best—with no opportunity for a second try—can determine whether they get the part in a film or television show or land a record deal. With so much on the line, and with only one chance to truly score, the survival instinct is typically at an all-time high. What's more, the audition experience often brings up issues of acceptance, validation, and judgment—the same issues anyone can face while working a room at a cocktail party, attending an important work or social function, or just trying to connect with someone new they're strongly attracted to. We all know what it's like to try to win people over, be they a director, a producer, or simply a potential mate. And since issues of judgment and rejection are major buttons for the survival instinct, fear can quickly undermine the entire endeavor. This is what happened to Janet, the part-time actress we met earlier who was at the mercy of her survival instinct. You may not be an aspiring actor, but chances are you have your own "auditions" to get through in life that have you needing to be "on." The secret is to be able to shine in the "on" mode without turning on your survival instinct.

Now let's consider Shannon. Shannon came to me after botching several key auditions for television parts. But Shannon wasn't new to the business. She had a long history of being successful in acting, and she'd had starring roles in several long-standing television series. Now in her mid-forties and up against younger actors, however, she found it harder to find roles and win auditions. She described to me that while under pressure to do well in her past few auditions, she made choices in her delivery of the script that sabotaged her performance. This happened in spite of the fact she could effectively deliver her lines effortlessly and expertly when she practiced at home and with her acting coach. Logically and after many years in the business, Shannon knew that auditions were not always about performance, and that other factors were involved, notably hair color, age, height, and general appearance. But knowing this did nothing to mitigate the fears that she felt. By the time she visited me, this fear of failing had reached stratospheric levels, as it was now compromising her abilities. Days before an audition Shannon would struggle to memorize and recall her lines, a problem that she'd never encountered before. Previously, all it took was one reading for her to commit a monologue to memory. Now, however, her survival instinct was in control, stripping her of skills she'd acquired long ago. Although it's natural to feel discomfort around auditions, which are inherently nerve-racking, for Shannon the audition experience had morphed into a personal threat. She had to train her brain how to manage her discomfort, to truly depersonalize it and experience it without letting it feel like a threat. Only then could she ultimately overcome her audition fears, and eventually get her next acting job.

Although Shannon was an actress, many of us can relate to situations that seem critical at the time—instead of performing like we want to, we find ourselves looking foolish or unattractive, at the worst possible time. We walk away from these situations feeling dreadful, saying to ourselves, "Why did I say that? Couldn't I have said this instead?"

This can happen in a variety of scenarios: with someone we've recently met and want to impress, with our boss when we want a promotion, or at a party where we feel nervous and uncomfortable, spilling our drink at the table. All these situations have one thing in common: a feeling of discomfort that is poorly managed and leads to unfulfilling consequences.

Grooming Yourself to Thrive Under Pressure

Let's now turn our attention to strategies that can be used not only to manage performance-related discomfort, but to boost performance as well. These will reiterate the methods I outlined in the previous chapter, as well as offer additional techniques you can apply to your life, no matter what kind of test or performance you face. Although it would be nice to work in a setting in which we are trained to manage discomfort, or to learn these skills in formal education, it's more realistic that we have to acquire them on our own. Part of my reason for including this chapter in the book is to help you do just that, with a secondary intention of motivating our leaders—school administrators, bosses, and parents—to begin implementing and/or supporting programs geared to help students and workers manage their discomfort better. After all, it's one of the surest ways of tapping into the true potential of students and workers in every type of circumstance, from formal classrooms and boardrooms to informal playgrounds and stages.

EMBRACE THE CHALLENGE

Recall that I covered how the power of challenge can go a long way toward improving resilience and hardiness in terms of discomfort. Robin, for instance, was able to use the power of challenge to transform his fear into productive performance. Remember, we are not interested in banishing discomfort; rather, like a Special Forces soldier or an elite athlete, we want to convert it into a catalyst that facilitates performance instead of hindering it.

I remember when Kobe Bryant was interviewed at the age of nineteen or twenty about how he felt about performing under pressure for the Lakers. It was common for him to be called into the game at the very end just so he could receive the ball and make a basket for the win. When he was asked about what it was like to be placed in such a position, he said, "This is when the game gets interesting and fun." So even at an early age, Kobe had already established the ability to embrace challenge in a healthy manner that would produce positive results.

Embracing discomfort as a challenge is something that can be learned and practiced. Where most individuals go wrong is in assuming that accepting challenge means not feeling discomfort.

The goal is not to pretend that discomfort doesn't exist; it's to find strategies to cope with it more effectively. So in teaching this strategy to students and workers, it is essential to help them understand this critical distinction.

FIND YOUR INNER GLADIATOR

The inner gladiator technique can work in tandem with embracing challenge. This technique is especially valuable if you don't view yourself as capable of handling adversity well. Although many people present themselves as confident and competent, the fact is many of those same people collapse under stressful or adverse conditions. This is when the fear of not being able to stand up to adversity gives adversity even more power. You may project an air of confidence and strength but feel weak or helpless in the face of crisis. You need to summon your inner gladiator.

In my clinical practice and groups I have conducted on test performance, having people imagine themselves as a particular person or fantasy character whom they equate with strength and fortitude can make embracing challenge even more successful. This is partly due to the fact that it's easier to attribute strength to someone other than yourself. And the inner gladiator technique takes your instinctual tendency toward weakness or failure under conditions of uncertainty and fear, and makes it easier for you to identify with an inner sense of strength. This technique takes the well-known *faking it until you make it* to a whole new level of brain community development.

SEEK SOCIAL SUPPORT

Remember, tapping into the power of social support is an important tool for managing all kinds of discomfort. Social support is an invaluable means of teaching workers and students how to manage their discomfort. This method was also espoused by Robin Richards in his use of creating heterogeneous teams that were taught to function in a cooperative atmosphere. All school and work settings would do well to encourage more team-based projects. This strategy has the added benefit of capitalizing on cooperation, which is proven to produce better results than competition. Unfortunately, this often conflicts with the way many of us were raised, given our cultural history: The pioneering spirit embraces the opposite—a competitive, independent individual. This is the ideology America was founded on, which explains why there's a natural tendency in our culture to "go it alone" and seek individual glory. And although it's true that competition can lead to great results for individuals striving for a prize, more often than not, the stakes are too high. Only a few people who choose to go it alone actually achieve what they want. In a world of interconnecting economies, cooperation and collaboration will ultimately produce the best performance results for the vast majority of people.

ASSUME RISK

Virtually everyone will say yes to the question "Do you want to be successful?" But why, then, do so many people settle for "just getting by" or giving up entirely? For many, what underlies this paradox is a fear of failure, and playing it safe and not giving their absolute best effort allows them to manage this fear. Not striving for success is a maladaptive habit, and such avoidance becomes a form of protection. Let me describe a case that illustrates this well.

Rachel was a thirty-nine-year-old executive with an MBA working in a high-pressure technology firm. Her typical workday lasted twelve hours, and weekends entailed work as well. Although she climbed the corporate ladder quickly, in the past couple of years she felt she had plateaued and was now being passed over for promotions and higher bonuses. When she came to me, she'd been struggling with an unrelenting fatigue, which crippled her ability to work late. Yet it couldn't be pinned on an underlying medical condition. But I learned through spending time with her that this fatigue, which was real, also served a different purpose: It gave her an out and a way of saving face in terms of being rejected for future promotions. In other words, she could avoid the risk of future rejections on the basis of being too enervated to pursue reviews and promotions. It was far less emotionally risky to forgo a job promotion due to an illness than it was to commit to the promotion process and be passed over—at which point she'd have to confront the fact that she wasn't as capable or as smart as her colleague who received the promotion.

Our fear of assuming such emotional risk at work can commonly materialize in a physical manner, like it did with Rachel. I call this condition Resistance to Health, and it's based on a study I conducted years ago on medical patients in the Psychoimmune Program I founded and directed at an L.A. hospital. In my previous book, *When Relaxation Is Hazardous to Your Health*, I explain how we can develop a resistance to becoming well, whereby our desire to avoid emotional discomfort can interfere with our ability to heal and sustain health. In a sense, ill health becomes a maladaptive habit and a practical means of escaping discomfort and risk in our lives.

Students may also take a course of action that is meant to shield them from emotional risk. Rather than committing to studying test material, they can easily be distracted by mindless Web surfing or eating when they aren't hungry as a way to avoid getting serious about their studying. And although on the surface it may seem as simple as poor work habits or procrastination, more often it is a way to blame their mediocre test performance on not having enough time to study as opposed to not being intelligent enough.

I have also seen the fear of assuming risk transpire outside of work, with respect to losing weight. In a clinical program I developed for chronic dieters, I help individuals control problem foods while breaking the connection between wanting to eat and their moods, such as boredom, anger, and fear. Unlike current methods, which direct their intervention to the cerebral brain, I designed my program to directly recondition the limbic brain's pleasure center through a process I call HypnoConditioning. Since the program influences the pleasure center directly, it particularly shines in several main areas: sustaining weight loss long-term, builiding inhibitions to problem and trigger foods, and creating satiation with smaller food portions.

For dieters in particular, the fear of risk surfaces in a very insidious way. For a certain subset of dieters, rather than emerging at the beginning of a weight loss journey, it tends to creep in after someone has lost a substantial amount of weight, such as forty or fifty pounds. Even though the weight loss has occurred relatively easily and with little discomfort, there is a point that certain individuals come to where they just plateau and seem to lose their desire to go further (e.g., if their goal is to lose sixty or seventy pounds). When I explore this shift in them, I encounter statements like "I have done enough for now; I can live with this." Essentially, a commanding and nearly hidden voice within them says that they are done pursuing the path of change, even though their level of discomfort has been minimal. Despite their success, there is a hidden fear that lurks within them, and it is often a fear of failure. And somehow not achieving their ultimate weight loss goal serves a protective function for them—much in the same way Rachel's fatigue did for her.

As we can see, the need to play it safe can take an enormous toll on our work and school performance, as well as our health. Although it may save face and provide some semblance of safety, it's terribly undermining in terms of our future performance and self-development. Training to assume risk should begin in our schools, where we can teach young students to embrace calculated risks as opposed to all the emphasis being placed on success alone. In the real world of achievement, only successes are rewarded, while failures are not. When I say "failures" I'm referring to failed outcomes from valiant attempts and calculated risk-taking. If a child takes a chance on trying something new and innovative, but it doesn't pan out well, then his efforts should be acknowledged in a way that encourages him to try again (note that this is different from excessively rewarding individuals to the extent that they expect accolades all the time). Such saluting of efforts can ultimately contribute to much higher levels of performance while lessening the need to play it safe. It can also spur the kind of innovation we all would like to see in our schools and companies.

PUT THE HEAT ON

One of the best strategies for managing fear related to performance pressure is to practice problem solving under time constraints. Even if we don't need to actually work against a clock, performance under pressure can help us hone our skills. A natural tendency is to want to practice in a comfortable setting or manner, but the real world constantly reminds us that ideal environments seldom occur. Recall the example in the previous chapter about duality, in which my patients who learned to relax and stay focused despite noisy distractions were much more prepared for the real world. The same is true of performance: The more we can practice performing in real-life conditions with plenty of distractions and time constraints, the more likely the discomfort we feel while under pressure becomes *facilitative*. We can hold the survival instinct at bay.

For individuals looking to excel in their academic pursuits, I often have them practice actual test questions under significant time constraints that are far more pressing than the actual time constraints of the exam. For example, I have lawyers take multiple-choice questions from the bar exam or formulate their answers to the essay questions at a very rapid pace. The goal of this exercise, however, is not necessarily accuracy. Instead it's to develop a greater comfort in high-pressure, high-stakes conditions.

For those looking for improvement in their work environment, I have them start working on math problems against time. This offers a wonderful opportunity to practice feeling uncomfortable and learning to channel it in a constructive manner. The discomfort is evoked in two ways. First, math problems cause discomfort for a large segment of the population. Second, solving math problems under time constraints compounds these individuals' feelings of discomfort. In this exercise, the goal is not accuracy or the best score. Much to the contrary, the goal is simply to develop a comfort zone while under pressure.

The end result of practicing in these circumstances is that it truly grooms a mental and physical toughness, and an improved ability to manage discomfort. It also strengthens the association between discomfort and productive performance.

Grooming for Success

As I've been reiterating, we can groom and develop the skills to perform our best and make good decisions under pressure. For sure some people are instinctively better able to perform under strenuous conditions. But this represents a small percentage, and it isn't necessary to become as good as an elite athlete or Special

Forces soldier to truly harness your abilities. With respect to students, if the goal is to groom them for maximum performance and the ability to convert their academic knowledge into performance, then it makes far more sense to provide some skills training for our younger generations at an earlier age. Doing so would alleviate so much collateral damage caused by their discomfort, such as low self-esteem, avoiding risks that could prove lucrative, or giving up entirely. It would also improve students' ability to apply their knowledge to the real world.

But equally important is preparing workers who are employed by a company. To maximize profits and worker productivity, it makes sense to put in the time, effort, and money to develop workers' abilities to manage discomfort while performing their job duties under pressure. Not only would this maximize returns on employees, but it would also lead to far fewer expenses that are directly related to employees suffering on the job. Health insurance companies are leading the way by rewarding those companies whose employees have healthier lifestyles. It's pretty obvious that unhealthy lifestyles can be a factor of mismanaged discomfort. And it goes without saying that the healthier the employee is, the more productive and happy he or she ultimately is at work.

Trends in tougher work demands and higher expectations are likely here to stay. We have only two options: play or don't play. And if we decide to play, then we have no choice but to develop the skills that can manage the related discomfort over the long haul. Life is, after all, a marathon rather than a sprint. The best chance we have for living healthy, productive lives is to hone those skills that manage discomfort in the long run. And the good news is that there are now evidence-based methods that can make this possible.

Conclusion

Discomfort— An Opportunity for Growth

I was fascinated from a very early age by the ability to use the mind to influence the body. At thirteen years old I received a reel-to-reel tape recorder, and it was then that I had an opportunity to hear my singing voice. Like many kids of my generation, I was inspired by the Beatles and began playing guitar and singing around ten or eleven. But when I heard my singing voice on the tape recorder, I was astonished how off key it was.

I then came across a book on self-hypnosis that my mother had in her personal library. I read it with the hope I could use hypnosis to train myself to sing in tune, and then spent a long time using the techniques to improve my singing voice. Although I had some success, my early experience with hypnosis became the start of my passionate interest in using this tool to influence the mind and the body. Soon I began experimenting with it in the sports I was playing. By age sixteen, I was hypnotizing kids on the block who had learned of my interest in hypnosis, and by eighteen, I was hypnotizing kids going through final exams in college. It wasn't until I began my graduate studies that I initiated my formal training in hypnosis. My first foray into this technique as a graduate student in the seventies was to test it out on patients undergoing surgery, and I found that it worked wonders on their ability to recover quickly after an operation.

Of course, being a product of the sixties and seventies had me curious about exploring altered states of consciousness, and how these might influence experiences such as intuition, spiritualism, and other less tangible states. Working with several classmates in the biofeedback lab in graduate school, I experimented with altering brain rhythms with EEG feedback—creating alpha states, for example. Although it did have an interesting physical impact, mainly changing levels of relaxation and alertness, it didn't create a profound shift in consciousness. I ultimately found that hypnosis was far more powerful in creating mind-altering results—and it had the ability to alter physical states. Through hypnosis, it was possible to alter the interpretation and experience of the body's sensory input, inducing powerful physical sensations. I could make myself feel like I was floating, alter my visual perceptions, and create sweeping mood changes like those achieved by opiate drugs. I also could use hypnosis to induce a spiritual connection or a broader affinity with nature.

These experiences weren't confined to graduate school. As you likely figured out by now, I have spent much of my adult life exploring these higher levels of consciousness in myself and in those patients who seek me out for this purpose. I know how these various mental states can foster intuitiveness and a greater connection with one's higher self, whether that be a greater attunement or access to your inner resources or a universal connection with nature, God, or another large life force.

My whole point in sharing a few more details from my own life and experiences with mind-body work is to convey once more just how powerful the brain can be. It can be retrained to uproot unhealthy instincts. It can be rewired so that the body embraces new physical and emotional patterns that are productive and supportive of your best health. By developing new pathways we can open new doors to health and happiness. If you're still skeptical of any of this, then I hope that by implementing the strategies in this book starting today, you'll be able to appreciate the power of your own mind soon. So much is possible.

Pain with No Gain

It's important to distinguish between managed and unmanaged discomfort, a theme that I've been describing since the beginning of the book. Earlier I referred to the old adage "no pain, no gain," which could be interpreted to mean "that which doesn't kill me will strengthen me." In actuality, extensive adversity can be just as bad as none at all. In a 2011 study of the impact and value of adversity, researchers demonstrated that some lifetime hardship—but not extreme—is predictive of greater resilience. In other words, discomfort for the sake of discomfort is not what builds resilience or hardiness; rather, it's the ability to manage discomfort and grow from it that's critical. When suffering is doled out endlessly, it offers little chance to grow and develop, but instead ultimately leads to a conditioned powerlessness—regression and paralysis as opposed to progression. However, managed adversity and discomfort leads to growth and change. It's just like that old saying: Pain is inevitable, but suffering is not.

I'm a firm believer that the path of discomfort offers us so much more than comfort ever has. Discomfort may very well be the most powerful change agent we have in our arsenal for becoming all that we can be—and achieving the kind of success in life that we all want. As I mentioned earlier, this book was conceived and written while I was in the throes of some serious personal upheaval. Although I have worked for years assisting others besieged by discomfort, it was my own that provided the inspiration for this book. For more than thirty years I have crafted and used all the techniques for managing discomfort described here with clients who have allowed me to serve them in their time of need. Only more recently did science finally catch up and demonstrate how and why these strategies work and that they can truly change our experience of discomfort at the cellular and biochemical level. And little did I know that my experience in managing the discomfort of others would ultimately be of great service to me in my darkest hour.

I had no idea, until I found myself in this place, how spiraling discomfort could steal my life force and imprison my soul. I was so thankful that when I felt buried and seemingly overwhelmed by discomfort these approaches provided a ticket out of the darkness, a beam of light and a ray of hope when I needed it the most.

But these techniques were much more than a life preserver in choppy seas for me. What I've come to realize is that they are emblematic of a paradigm shift for experiencing and understanding discomfort. They open a door into a new galaxy of higher levels of consciousness. **Once discomfort becomes more manageable—a safe place to be—it becomes possible to learn what it truly has to offer.** Perhaps it requires a certain rite of passage, for I can't say I really grasped the value of vulnerability until I was faced with such seizing discomfort. Through the years I have assisted so many of my patients in their lowest points, and I had experienced the wounds of weakness before. But it wasn't until I made more and more peace with my own discomfort that I could create the sweeping changes in my life that I had put off for years, as well as find the strength to move forward.

Vulnerability for the sake of vulnerability isn't enough. It can be paralyzing, endless, a one-way street, and an escape. And at first for me, it felt like quicksand, entrapping and immobilizing. But as

I made my way through learning to manage my discomfort and feel a greater sense of safety within it, I found myself increasingly able to benefit from my own discomfort. So it was not the presence but rather the management of discomfort that made change and growth possible. And although it may seem counterintuitive, the pursuit of comfort can be destructive and deadly—we need some level of discomfort in our lives to grow, adapt, and change for the better. It can wake us up to life issues we need to address, behaviors we should alter, and resolutions or goals we would do well to make and achieve. When we try to live in a world where we demand and seek comfort, we inadvertently set ourselves up for stagnation, atrophy, and deterioration.

Yet discomfort is just that—uncomfortable, and as a result is strongly related to vulnerability. In *The Healing Power of Emotion*, psychiatrist and neuroscientist Daniel Siegel describes how vulnerability is something that our survival depends upon and discusses how it actually leads to wisdom, and ultimately to a better integration of the brain's various compartments and all of its resources. As with discomfort, there are many different degrees of vulnerability, some of which lead to only moderate levels of discomfort, while others spark overwhelming discomfort. But it's during all of these times that change can actually become more possible. Discomfort is arguably the most powerful change agent we have to expand our lives in unimaginable ways.

OUR TOLERANCE LEVELS FOR DISCOMFORT ARE MUCH GREATER THAN WE BELIEVE

I have consistently observed how our inherent capabilities are often far more expansive than we give ourselves credit for—particularly with respect to how well we can cope with discomfort. Paul Slovic, of the University of Oregon, is a leading theorist and researcher in the field of risk perception, which basically means he studies how we judge the characteristics and severity of each risk we face. In one particular study, Slovic noticed that the more benefits we attribute to a technology, the lower the amount of risk we perceive in that technology. This is particularly true today with respect to the popularity of risky medical procedures such as cosmetic surgery and gastric bypass operations. These are high-tech procedures that bear a lot of risks, but people perceive the benefits as outweighing those risks. The pros of the promised results (a thinner, more beautiful you) weigh heavier than the cons of going under the knife (side effects, the risk of a botched surgery). Slovic's observation has everything to do with the subject of discomfort. **Simply stated, the more benefit we attach to discomfort, the more we can come to perceive it with less fear, as less risky, and as being an asset to protect.** We can, in essence, embrace discomfort as a necessary evil in our journey to live better, more enriching lives. One of the important goals of this book has been to present the discomfort experience in a brand new light.

Clearly, this book has also addressed our shrinking comfort zone. But in reality, we have a far greater ability to tolerate discomfort than we think. As I've been emphasizing, the human species has persevered through millennia by tolerating trials and tribulations, and thriving no matter what. In fact, studies of willpower by Veronika Job and her team at Stanford have determined that willpower is limited only if you believe it is. If, however, you believe willpower is "self-renewing," then your tolerance for resisting temptation and dealing with discomfort becomes much greater. This has huge applications for our ability to manage discomfort, because **in most cases, we are much more capable of dealing with discomfort than we've been taught to believe in our present culture.**

PREPARING THE NEXT GENERATION

As you can imagine, most of the people who come to see me are at a crisis point in their lives, be it physical or emotional. Obviously, I don't want you to reach the proverbial rock bottom before you begin to manage your agitance better and tolerate more discomfort so you can turn your life around. It's not necessary for someone to undergo significant emotional travail in order to reap all the benefits that I've covered. Perhaps a broader question that needs to be asked about our culture, however, relates to our drive to continually add greater creature comforts to our lives.

Does our urge to create more comforts undermine our long-term interests in evolving into a society that is far more hardy and resilient? I suspect you may know the answer to this question by now. And we in fact see this revealing itself with our children, many of whom appear to be growing up not only with greater comforts than previous generations ever had, but also with higher levels of agitance. Kids today are constantly being shuffled from one activity to another—rushing to soccer practice after school, then home in time for piano lessons followed by their math tutor, ending the day in a mad dash to complete their homework assignments before bedtime, which can be delayed as a result. Where's the downtime for this younger generation? Is it any surprise that they struggle with idleness or lack of structure, and grow up craving high levels of stimulation? Is it any wonder attention deficit hyperactivity disorder is at an all-time high? From a clinical standpoint, I am witnessing in my practice a growing number of children developing symptoms and conditions related to soaring levels of unmanaged agitance and a survival instinct on alert like a crouching tiger. I know that my colleagues are seeing this as well.

Indeed, the problem has strong implications for parenthood. Parents have an innate desire to protect their children from harm or the same traumas we experienced in childhood. A personal case in point: When my daughter was just three or four, while on a picnic with her twin brother and a boy who went to the same preschool, the boy came up to my son and daughter and said, "Let's go check out that hill over there." Both my son and daughter stood up to join him. But the boy turned to my daughter and said, "Girls can't come; this is only for boys." My daughter froze, and I knew exactly what had happened: For the first time in her life, she felt a sense of rejection. I felt helpless to stop it and I could see she was shattered inside, as tears rolled down her face. I tried to comfort her, but it didn't erase the pain of her first rejection. I instantly felt sad and upset, but I also felt that I'd let my child down by not being able to protect her from the disappointments and coldness of the outside world. And of course this was my instinctual parental response.

Others have written extensively on the topic of "over-parenting"—of taking too much responsibility for our children and being far more protective of them than we should. I tend to agree that we over-parent today, because it's not just about teaching our kids to fend for themselves and succeed on their own—more than anything it's about training them to manage their own discomfort. We can help our children learn to confront their discomfort rather than embracing futility or looking for short-term solutions, and to accept that it is something they can learn to skillfully control and parlay into future life successes. Simply stated, teaching children how to experience discomfort while feeling safe at the same time may very well be the greatest gift we can give them as parents.

A Safe Passage Awaits You

Recently, while attending a family function, I met a cute seven-year-old boy with a nice smile. He was the son of a young mother whom I hadn't seen for a number of years. When the boy gave me a quick smile, I picked him up and lifted him in the air as a gesture of kindness and good-spirited fun. He quickly said, "I don't like this," so I immediately returned him to the ground. But once he was grounded he then said, "That was really fun!" And then added, "But I don't want to do it again right now."

To me, this was an excellent example of how early our fears take hold of our lives. Without retraining the brain and body, we can inadvertently become enslaved by those fears for the rest of our lives. In this particular case, the boy's reaction is a perfect example of what typically happens when we are confronted with being uncomfortable. Our gut reaction is to say, "Stop." But then we might notice that there was something redeeming about it. Yet, we find ourselves resisting it in the future. How often does this happen when people lose a great deal of weight or get themselves in better physical shape? It so frequently doesn't hold, and people revert to a previous level of comfort.

And this is exactly what happens to so many of us when confronted with discomfort. The survival instinct kicks in and we choose to pull back and unconsciously stop ourselves from being able to explore and embrace new ways of being, whether it relates to intimacy with a partner, advancement in our career, taking action to boost our health, or exploring the higher levels of our potential. Put simply, we choose to let our survival instinct run our lives—and in some cases, run *over* our lives.

Native Americans and other early tribal cultures were half-right in believing that it was necessary to endure significant physical pain as a rite of passage—learning that they could endure pain and still manage to survive. And no doubt physical pain does challenge our inner fears. But I've learned in my years of practice and in my own personal experience that emotional pain can be far more challenging than physical pain. Physical pain is usually limited to a specific part of the body, while emotional pain feels all encompassing, with no way to quarantine it. It's no surprise, then, that the survival instinct is so quick to act to protect us when it perceives potential emotional harm and danger. And as long as our survival instinct rushes to stand up and shield us from anticipated emotional pain, we find ourselves entrapped by our instinctual primitive responses, such as anger, paralysis, overeating, illness, aggression, and withdrawal.

But by tolerating greater emotional distress without turning to the survival instinct for protection, we find that this does indeed become a doorway into exploring and developing our true potential, as well as higher evolved states of consciousness in which our intuition, connection, and spiritualism thrive. **These higher evolved states really don't happen without us learning that we can walk through emotional rings of fire without being burned.** And maybe that's just it—to really develop these higher levels of experience, the brain, body, and even the soul (if you believe in a soul or spirit) must know that whatever information and experience is received, no matter how uncomfortable, can be handled and managed in a safe manner. And if you don't feel this safety, then there is little chance of being able to receive or embrace these evolved states of consciousness with greater consistency.

And so I come to the crux of the matter: **Discomfort or vulnerability in our present day actually has more survival value than being comfortable once had in prehistoric times.** Seeking and settling for comfort and familiarity now leads to rigidity and a constriction of brain resources. Although our ancient wiring strives for familiarity and comfort because it allowed us to survive in the past, today it actually impedes our ability to function and age more successfully. After all, aging is nothing more than a reflection of our behaviors and habits, as well as how we choose to preside over what we confront in life.

Which brings me to where I began this book. The management of discomfort is the single most important skill for the twenty-first century. Whether your goal is improvement in work performance, health, or relationships, or higher levels of being, they are all ultimately contingent on developing a higher threshold of discomfort while relying less on the survival instinct to keep you safe. In this next century, our overly engaged survival instinct will be our biggest obstacle to finding health and happiness, and it will hold us back from exploring other areas that make life worth living.

The survival instinct is truly our inner gatekeeper, separating us from our animalistic past and from our potentially more highly evolved selves. So becoming comfortable with being uncomfortable and vulnerable really is the most important tool in the twenty-first century. Once you form this new relationship and partnership with discomfort, the survival instinct will be relegated to where it is truly needed. Any remaining obstacles will be far less formidable and much more manageable.

All of this is within our reach, and with discomfort as our partner, we can go far.

Acknowledgments

I knew at the outset of this project in April of 2011 that its success would ultimately depend on a team effort. My instincts proved right, and it is for this reason that I have great appreciation and gratitude for my family, friends, and colleagues who have made a contribution. I have many of you to thank for your substantive suggestions and ideas. But equally important and meaningful are those of you whose contribution was non-substantive.

I begin first with my two greatest loves of all time, my children, Meriah and Nathan, without whom I never would have experienced and understood what it means to love unconditionally, or been able to fully grasp the meaning of loss.

My biggest thank-you of all goes out to my two brothers, Darryl and Dennis, who have made such an incredible difference in my life and have been an enduring pillar of support, strength, and wisdom every step of the way.

I offer my sincerest appreciation and gratitude for my lifelong friends, Jeff and Liz Kramer, for their love, generosity, support, and kindness, and a special thank-you to my longtime friend Jeff Lerman.

I would like to deeply thank my good friends, Drs. John Milliman and Mark Weisberg, for your long-term friendship, insights, laughs, and our journeys in nature.

I feel enormous appreciation for the contribution of my writing partner, Kristin Loberg. Kristin, you have truly put your heart and soul into this project, and have been instrumental on so many levels. In the early stages of this project it was truly a labor of love, where at times it felt as if we were lost and wandering in the desert, with no certainty of finding a homeland. Yet your commitment was unshakable. Your writing skills, intelligence, patience, passion, warm heart, positive attitude, and very importantly, your friendship, have been invaluable in refining my message and creating this book. I can't imagine having done this without you.

I truly owe the existence of this book to my literary agent, Bonnie Solow. Bonnie, this never would have happened if you had not persuasively reached out to me. Thank you for finding a book in me that I didn't know existed, and for all your edits, input, vision, and for skillfully shepherding this book to fruition. Without you I never would have set foot on a path that opened up so many doors for emotional and intellectual growth and solace.

I would also like to acknowledge the outstanding contribution of my editor, Meghan Stevenson, who brought so much zest, spirit, and personal interest in this project. Your edits and suggestions have had a very significant and positive impact on this book's readability, organization, and message. Please accept an additional thank-you for your generosity in granting me so much editorial freedom.

My acknowledgments would not be complete without extending a very big thank-you to Caroline Sutton; without her, this project would never have happened at Hudson Street. Thank you for your swift acceptance and welcome into the Penguin Hudson Street family, and for believing in a body of work that was still yet to be fleshed out and refined.

I also would like to offer a thank-you to Kym Surridge, Penguin's copy editor, who was simply amazing and brilliant in making critical edits and tightening up this manuscript. And to Brittney Ross, who helped carry this book through its final phase of production.

Finally, I would like to thank you, the reader, for taking an interest in my work and life passion. I truly hope it provides you with opportunities for new growth and solace, much in the same way as it has for me through the years.

Selected Bibliography

The following is a partial list of books and scientific papers that you might find helpful in learning more about some of the ideas and concepts expressed in this book. This is by no means an exhaustive list, but it features many of the studies mentioned in the book and will get you started in embracing the principles I've detailed. These materials can also open other doors for further research and inquiry. For access to more studies and an ongoing, updated list of references, please visit www.marcschoen.com. If you do not see a reference listed here that was mentioned in the book, please refer to the website, where a more comprehensive list is found.

Chapter 2

National Center for Health Statistics at the Center for Disease Control and Prevention's website for facts on population health: www.cdc.gov/nchs/. Note that these numbers tend to change or be reported differently by other organizations; for example, in the fall of 2011, the Commonwealth Fund reported that the United States placed last among sixteen high-income, industrialized nations when it comes to deaths that could potentially have been prevented by timely access to effective health care. You can access this particular finding at www.commonwealthfund.org

and search for the following: "New Study: U.S. Ranks Last Among High-Income Nations on Preventable Deaths, Lagging Behind as Others Improve More Rapidly."

World Health Organization website for facts on depression: http://www.who.int/mental_health/management/depression/definition/en/ (accessed June 19, 2012).

Chapter 3

Eisenberger, J. L., and M. D. Lieberman. "Why rejection hurts: A common neural alarm system for physical and social pain." *Trends in Cognitive Science* 8 (2004): 294–300.

Seery, M. D. "Resilience: A silver lining to experiencing adverselife events?" *Current Directions in Psychological Science* 20, no. 6 (Dec. 2011): 390–94.

Chapter 4

Blumenthal, D. M., and M. S. Gold. "Neurobiology of food addiction." *Current Opinion in Clinical Nutrition and Metabolic Care* 13, no. 4 (July 2010): 359–65.

Bowling S. L., and M. T. Bardo . "Locomotor and rewarding effects of amphetamine in enriched, social, and isolate reared rats." *Pharmacology Biochemistry and Behavior* 48, no. 2 (June 1994): 459–64.

Bowling S. L., J. K. Rowlett, and M. T. Bardo. "The effect of environmental enrichment on amphetamine-stimulated locomotor activity, dopamine synthesis and dopamine release." *Neuropharmacology* 32, no. 9 (Sep. 1993): 885–93.

Gambarana, C., F. Masi, A. Tagliamonte, et al. "A chronic stress that impairs reactivity in rats also decreases dopaminergic transmission in the nucleus accumbens: A microdialysis study." *Neurochemistry* 72, no. 5 (1999): 2039–46.

Hebb, D. O. *The organization of behavior: A neuropsychological theory.* Psychology Press (New Edition), 2002. Originally published in 1949.

LeDoux, J. "The emotional brain, fear, and the amygdala." *Cellular and Molecular Neurobiology* 23 (2003): 727–38.

LeDoux, J. E. "Emotion circuits in the brain." *Annual Review of Neuroscience* 23 (2000): 155–84.

Lewis, M. D. "Bridging emotion theory and neurobiology through dynamic systems modeling." *Behavioral and Brain Science* 28, no. 2 (Apr. 2005): 169–94; discussion 194–245.

McGowan, P. O., and M. Szyf. "The epigenetics of social adversity in early life: Implications for mental health outcomes." *Neurobiology of Disease* 39, no. 1 (July 2010): 66–72. Epub Jan. 4, 2010.

McGowan, P. O., et al. "Epigenetic regulation of the glucocorticoid receptor in human brain associates with childhood abuse." *Nature Neuroscience* 12, no. 3 (March 2009): 342–48.

Meaney, M. J., and A. C. Ferguson-Smith. "Epigenetic regulation of the neural transcriptome: The meaning of the marks." *Nature Neuroscience* 13, no. 11 (2010): 1313–18.

Meaney, M. J., and M. Szyf. "Maternal care as a model for experience-dependent chromatin plasticity?" *Trends in Neurosciences* 28, no. 9 (Sep. 2005): 456–63.

Miller, G. "The invisible wounds of war. Healing the brain, healing the mind." *Science* 333, no. 6042 (July 2011): 514–17.

Mograbi, G. J. "Meditation and the brain: Attention, control and emotion." *Mens Sana Monographs* 9, no. 1 (2011): 276–83.

Morgan, D., et al. "Social dominance in monkeys: Dopamine D2 receptors and cocaine self-administration." *Nature Neuroscience* 5, no. 2 (Feb. 2002): 169–74.

Morrison, S. E, and C. D. Salzman. "Re-valuing the amygdala." *Current Opinion in Neurobiology* 20, no. 2 (Apr. 2010): 221–30. Epub Mar. 17, 2010.

Mysels, D. J., and M. A. Sullivan. "The relationship between opioid and sugar intake: Review of evidence and clinical applications." *Journal of Opioid Management* 6, no. 6 (Nov.–Dec. 2010): 445–52.

Olivier, George, Sandy Ghozland, Marc R. Azar, et al. "CRF–CRF1 system activation mediates withdrawal-induced increases in nicotine self-administration in nicotine-dependent rats." *Proceedings of the National Academy of Sciences* 104, no. 43 (Oct. 23, 2007).

Pare, D., G. J. Quirk, and J. E. LeDoux. "New vistas on amygdala networks in conditioned fear." *Journal of Neurophysiology* 92 (2004): 1–9.

Shin, L. M., et al. "A functional magnetic resonance imaging study of amygdala and medial prefrontal cortex responses to overtly presented fearful faces in posttraumatic stress disorder." *Archives of General Psychiatry* 62, no. 3 (Mar. 2005): 273–81.

Smith, M. A., P. A. Bryant, and J. M. McClean. "Social and environmental enrichment enhances sensitivity to the effects of kappa opioids: Studies on antinociception, diuresis and conditioned place preference." *Pharmacology, Biochemistry, and Behavior* 76 (2003): 93–101.

Stice, E., S. Yokum, K. Blum, and C. Bohon. "Weight gain is associated with reduced striatal response to palatable food." *Journal of Neuroscience* 30, no. 39 (Sep. 2010): 13105–9.

Wang, G. J., et al. "Evidence of gender differences in the ability to inhibit brain activation elicited by food stimulation." *Proceedings of the National Academy of Sciences* 106, no. 4 (Jan. 2009): 1249–54.

Warnick, J. E. "Propranolol and its potential inhibition of positive posttraumatic growth." *American Journal of Bioethics* 7, no. 9 (Sep. 2007): 37–38.

Wilensky, A. E., G. E. Schafe, and J. E. LeDoux. "Functional inactivation of the amygdala before but not after auditory fear conditioning prevents memory formation." *Journal of Neuroscience* 19, RC48 (1999).

Chapter 5

National Sleep Foundation: www.sleepfoundation.org.

Chapter 6

Ader, R., and N. Cohen. "Behaviorally conditioned immunosuppression and murine systemic lupus erythematosus." *Science* 215, no. 4529 (Mar. 1982): 1534–36.

Fitzsimons, G. M., T. L. Chartrand, and G. J. Fitzsimons. "Automatic effects of brand exposure on motivated behavior: How Apple makes you 'think different.'" *Journal of Consumer Research* 35, no. 1 (June 2008): 21–35.

Johnson, A. W., M. Gallagher, and P. C. Holland. "The basolateral amygdala is critical to the expression of Pavlovian and instrumental outcome-specific reinforcer devaluation effects. *The Journal of Neuro-*

science 29, no. 3 (Jan. 2009): 696–704; doi:10.1523/JNEUROSCI.3758-08.2009.

Johnston, L. "Behavioral mimicry and stigmatization." *Social Cognition* 20 (2002): 18–35.

Mazar, N., and C. B. Zhong. "Do green products make us better people?" *Psychological Science: A Journal of the American Psychological Society* 21, no. 4 (2002): 494–98; PMID: 20424089.

McElrea, H., and F. Standing. "Fast music causes fast drinking." *Perceptual and Motor Skills* 75 (1992): 362.

Patton, C. J. "Fear of abandonment and binge eating. A subliminal psychodynamic activation investigation." *Journal of Nervous and Mental Disease* 180, no. 8 (Aug. 1992): 484–90.

Schoen, M. *When relaxation is hazardous to your health: Why we get sick after the stress is over, and what you can do now to protect your health.* Mind Body Health Books, 2001.

Strahan, E. J., S. J. Spencer, and M. P. Zanna. "Subliminal priming and persuasion: Striking while the iron is hot." *Journal of Experimental Social Psychology* 38 (2002): 556–68.

Stroebel, N., and J. Castro. "Listening to music while eating is related to increases in people's food intake and meal duration." *Appetite* 47, no. 3 (Nov. 2006): 285–89.

Tanner, R. J., et al. "Of chameleons and consumption: The impact of mimicry on choice and preferences." *Journal of Consumer Research* 34 (2008): 754–67.

Zhong, C. B., and S. E. Devoe. "You are how you eat: Fast food and impatience." *Psychological Science: A Journal of the American Psychological Society* 21, no. 5 (2010): 619–22; PMID: 20483836. See also: http://www.ionpsych.com/2011/02/04/want-to-read-faster-think-more-creatively-and-be-a-better-person-buy-more-brand-name-stuff/ (accessed July 2, 2012).

Chapter 7

Bahrami, B., N. Lavie, and G. Rees. "Attentional load modulates responses of human primary visual cortex to invisible stimuli." *Current Biology* 17, no. 6 (Mar. 2007): 509–13. Epub Mar. 8, 2007. See also: University

College London (Mar. 8, 2007). "Subliminal advertising leaves its mark on the brain." *ScienceDaily.* Retrieved July 3, 2012, from http://www.sciencedaily.com /releases/2007/03/070308121938.htm.

Hjortskov, N., et al. "The effect of mental stress on heart rate variability and blood pressure during computer work." *European Journal of Applied Physiology* 92, nos. 1–2 (June 2004): 84–89. Epub Feb. 27, 2004.

Linden, D. *The compass of pleasure: How our brains make fatty foods, orgasm, exercise, marijuana, generosity, vodka, learning, and gambling feel so good.* New York: Viking, 2011.

Routtenberg, A., and J. Lindy. "Effects of the availability of rewarding septal and hypothalamic stimulation on bar pressing for food under conditions of deprivation." *Journal of Comparative and Physiological Psychology* 60, no. 2 (Oct. 1965): 158–61. See also: http://wings.buffalo.edu/aru/ARUreport01.htm (accessed July 5, 2012).

Chapter 8

Agus, D. B. *The end of illness.* New York: Free Press, 2012.

Bradley, R. T., et al. "Emotion self-regulation, psychophysiological coherence, and test anxiety: Results from an experiment using electrophysiological measures." *Applied Psychophysiology and Biofeedback* 35, no. 4 (Dec. 2010): 261–83.

Brasel, S. A., and J. Gips. "Media multitasking behavior: Concurrent television and computer usage." *Cyberpsychology, Behavior, and Social Networking* 14, no. 9 (Sep. 2011): 527–34. Epub Mar. 7, 2011.

Brydon, L., et al., "Hostility and cellular aging in men from the Whitehall II cohort." *Biological Psychiatry* 71, no. 9 (May 2012): 767–73.

Dutton, D. G., and A. Aron. "Some evidence for heightened sexual attraction under condtions of high anxiety." *Journal of Personality and Social Psychology* 30, no. 4 (Oct. 1974): 510–17.

Immordino-Yang, M. H., and A. Damasio. "We feel, therefore we learn: The relevance of affective and social neuroscience to education." *Mind, Brain, and Education* 1, no. 1 (2007): 3–10.

Jerath, R., J. W. Edry, V. A. Barnes, and V. Jerath. "Physiology of long pranayamic breathing: Neural respiratory elements may provide a mechanism that explains how slow deep breathing shifts the autonomic nervous system." *Medical Hypotheses* 67, no. 3 (2006): 566–71. Epub Apr. 18, 2006.

Lieberman, M. D., et al. "Putting feelings into words: Affect labeling disrupts amygdala activity in response to affective stimuli." *Psychological Science* 18, no. 5 (2007): 421–28.

Lutz, A., et al. "Attention regulation and monitoring meditation." *Trends in Cognitive Science* 12, no. 4 (Apr. 2008): 163–69. Epub Mar. 10, 2008.

Newberg, A. B., and J. Iversen. "The neural basis of the complex mental task of meditation: neurotransmitter and neurochemical considerations." *Medical Hypotheses* 61, no. 2 (Aug. 2003): 282–91.

Spielberger, C. D., and P. R. Vagg (eds.). *Test anxiety: Theory, assessment, and treatment.* Washington, DC: Taylor & Francis, 1995.

Steele, C. M., and J. Aronson. "Stereotype threat and the intellectual test performance of African-Americans." *Journal of Personality and Social Psychology* 69, no. 5 (Nov. 1995): 797–811.

Toussaint, L. L., A. D. Owen, and A. Cheadle. "Forgive to live: Forgiveness, health, and longevity." *Journal of Behavioral Medicine* 35, no. 4 (Aug. 2012): 375–86. Epub June 25, 2011.

Weinberg, R. S., and D. Gould. *Foundations of sport and exercise psychology*, 4th ed. Champaign, IL: Human Kinetics, 2007.

Wood, A. M., J. J. Froh, and A. W. Geraghty. "Gratitude and well-being: A review and theoretical integration." *Clinical Psychology Review* 30, no. 7 (Nov. 2010): 890–905. Epub Mar. 20, 2010.

Zeidner, M. *Test anxiety: The state of the art.* New York: Plenum Press, 1998.

Chapter 9

Bickart, K. C., et al. "Amygdala volume and social network size in humans." *Nature Neuroscience* 14, no. 2 (Feb. 2011): 163–64. Epub Dec. 26, 2010.

Dutton, D. G., and A. P. Aron. "Some evidence for heightened sexual attraction under conditions of high anxiety." *Journal of Personality and Social Psychology* 30, no. 4 (Oct. 1974): 510–17.

Emmons, R. A., and M. E. McCullough. "Counting blessings versus burdens: An experimental investigation of gratitude and subjective well-being in daily life." *Journal of Personality and Social Psychology* 84, no. 2 (Feb. 2003): 377–89.

Esch, T., and G. B. Stefano. "Endogenous reward mechanisms and their importance in stress reduction, exercise and the brain." *Archives of Medical Science* 6, no. 3 (June 2010): 447–55.

———. "The neurobiological link between compassion and love." *Medical Science Monitor* 17, no. 3 (Feb. 2011): RA65–75.

———. "The neurobiology of love." *Neuroendocrinology Letters* 26, no. 3 (June 2005): 175–92.

———. "The neurobiology of stress management." *Neuroendocrinology Letters* 31, no. 1 (2010): 19–39.

Frattaroli, J. "Experimental disclosure and its moderators: A meta-analysis." *Psychological Bulletin* 132, no. 6 (Nov. 2006): 823–65.

Geraghty, A. W., A. M. Wood, and M. E. Hyland. "Attrition from self-directed interventions: Investigating the relationship between psychological predictors, intervention content and dropout from a body dissatisfaction intervention." *Social Science and Medicine* 71, no. 1 (July 2010): 30–37. Epub Mar. 23, 2010.

Kéri S., I. Kiss, and O. Kelemen. "Sharing secrets: Oxytocin and trust in schizophrenia." *Society for Neuroscience* 4, no. 4 (2009): 287–93. Epub Aug. 1, 2008.

Kirsch, P., et al. "Oxytocin modulates neural circuitry for social cognition and fear in humans." *Journal of Neuroscience* 25, no. 49 (Dec. 7, 2005): 11489–93.

Kornfield, J. *The wise heart: A guide to the universal teachings of Buddhist psychology.* New York: Bantam, 2008.

Kosfeld, M., et al. Oxytocin increases trust in humans. *Nature* 435, no. 7042 (June 2005): 673–76.

Lazara, S. W., et al. "Meditation experience is associated with increased cortical thickness." *Neuroreport* 16, no. 17 (Nov. 28, 2005): 1893–97.

Lieberman, M. D., et al. "Putting feelings into words: Affect labeling disrupts amygdala activity in response to affective stimuli." *Psychological Science* 18, no. 5 (May 2007): 421–28.

Lieberman, M. D., T. K. Inagaki, G. Tabibnia, and M. J. Crockett. "Subjective responses to emotional stimuli during labeling, reappraisal, and distraction." *Emotion* 11, no. 3 (June 2011): 468–80.

Maddi, S. R. "The story of hardiness: Twenty years of theorizing, research and practice." *Consulting Psychology Journal* 54 (2002): 173–85.

Master, S. L., et al. "A picture's worth: Partner photographs reduce experimentally induced pain." *Psychological Science* 20, no. 11 (Nov. 2009): 1316–18. Epub Sep. 24, 2009.

Ozbay, F., H. Fitterling, D. Charney, and S. Southwick. "Social support and resilience to stress across the life span: A neurobiologic framework." *Current Psychiatry Reports* 10, no. 4 (Aug. 2008): 304–10.

Pennebaker, J. W., and S. K. Beall. "Confronting a traumatic event: Toward an understanding of inhibition and disease." *Journal of Abnormal Psychology* 95, no. 3 (Aug. 1986): 274–81.

Ramirez, G., and S. L. Beilock. "Writing about testing worries boosts exam performance in the classroom." *Science* 331, no. 6014 (Jan. 14, 2011): 211–13. See also: "The right stuff for test anxiety: Students score higher after jotting down worries before a big exam." *Science News* 179, no. 4 (Feb. 12, 2011): 9.

Schoen, M., and K. Nowack. "Reconditioning the stress response with hypnosis CD reduces the inflammatory cytokine 116 and influences resilience: A pilot study." *Complementary Therapies in Clinical Practice* (2013), in press.

Stefano, G. B., J. M. Stefano, and T. Esch. "Anticipatory stress response: A significant commonality in stress, relaxation, pleasure and love responses." *Medical Science Monitor* 14, no. 2 (Feb. 2008): RA17–21.

Stellar, J. E., V. M. Manzo, M. W. Kraus, and D. Keltner. "Class and compassion: Socioeconomic factors predict responses to suffering." *Emotion* 12, no. 3 (June 2012): 449–59. Epub Dec. 12, 2011. See also: "Lower classes quicker to show compassion in the face of suffering" by Yasmin Anwar on December 19, 2011, at http://newscenter.berkeley.edu/2011/12/19/classandincome/ (accessed July 5, 2012).

Szabolcs, K., and I. Kiss. "Oxytocin response in a trust game and habituation of arousal." *Physiology and Behavior* 102, no. 2 (2011): 221–24.

Tucker, D. M., P. Luu, and D. Derryberry. "Love hurts: The evolution of empathic concern through the encephalization of nociceptive capacity." *Development and Psychopathology* 17, no. 3 (Summer 2005): 699–713.

Vaillant, G. E. "The neuroendocrine system and stress, emotions, thoughts and feelings." *Mens Sana Monographs* 9, no. 1 (2011): 113–28.

Wood, A. M., J. J. Froh, and A.W. Geraghty. "Gratitude and well-being: A review and theoretical integration." *Clinical Psychology Review* 30, no. 7 (Nov. 2010): 890–905. Epub Mar. 20, 2010.

Zahn, R., et al. "The neural basis of human social values: Evidence from functional MRI." *Cerebral Cortex* 19, no. 2 (Feb. 2009): 276–83. Epub May 22, 2008.

Zak, P. J., R. Kurzban, and W. T. Matzner. "The neurobiology of trust." *Annals of the New York Academy of Sciences* 1032 (Dec. 2004): 224–27.

———. "Oxytocin is associated with human trustworthiness." *Hormones and Behavior* 48, no. 5 (Dec. 2005): 522–27. Epub Aug. 18, 2005.

Chapter 10

Anderson, S. W., et al. "Impairment of social and moral behavior related to early damage in human prefrontal cortex." *Nature Neuroscience* 2, no. 11 (Nov. 1999): 1032–37.

Baumeister, R., E. Bratslavsky, C. Finkenauer, and K. Vohs. "Bad is stronger than good." *Review of General Psychology* 5, no. 4 (2001): 323–70.

Bechara, A. "Decision making, impulse control and loss of willpower to resist drugs: A neurocognitive perspective." *Nature Neuroscience* 8, no. 11 (Nov. 2005): 1458–63.

Bechara, A., H. Damasio, D. Tranel, and A. R. Damasio. "Deciding advantageously before knowing the advantageous strategy." *Science* 275, no. 5304 (Feb. 1997): 1293–95.

Bradley, R. T., et al. "Emotion self-regulation, psychophysiological coherence, and test anxiety: Results from an experiment using electrophysiological measures." *Applied Psychophysiology and Biofeedback* 35, no. 4 (Dec. 2010): 261–83.

Hartley, E., and E. Phelp. "Anxiety and decision making." *Biological Psychiatry* 72 (2012): 113–18.

Kahneman, D. *Thinking, fast and slow.* New York: FSG Books, 2011.

Kahneman, D., and A. Tversky. "Prospect theory: An analysis of decisions under risk." *Econometrica* 47 (1979): 263–91.

Morgan, C. A. III, et al. "Hormone profiles in humans experiencing military survival training." *Biological Psychiatry* 47, no. 10 (May 15, 2000): 891–901.

Rozin, P., and E. B. Royzman. "Negativity bias, negativity dominance, and contagion." *Personality and Social Psychology Review* 5, no. 4 (2001): 296–320.

Schoen, Marc. "Resistance to health: When the mind interferes with the desire to become well." *American Journal of Clinical Hypnosis* 36, no. 1 (1993): 47–53.

Szafranski, D. D., T. L. Barrera, and P. J. Norton. "Test anxiety inventory: 30 years later." *Anxiety Stress Coping* (Feb. 7, 2012; Epub ahead of print).

Tse, M. T., A. Cantor, and S. B. Floresco. "Repeated amphetamine exposure disrupts dopaminergic modulation of amygdala-prefrontal circuitry and cognitive/emotional functioning." *Journal of Neuroscience* 31, no. 31 (Aug. 3, 2011): 11282–94.

Vaccaro, C. "Male bodies in manhood acts: The role of body-talk and embodied practice in signifying culturally dominant notions of manhood." *Sociology Compass* 5, no. 1 (2011): 65–76.

Yehuda, R., S. Brand, and R. K. Yang. "Plasma neuropeptide Y concentrations in combat exposed veterans: Relationship to trauma exposure, recovery from PTSD, and coping." *Biological Psychiatry* 59, no. 7 (Apr. 2006): 660–63. Epub Dec. 1, 2005.

Zeidner, M. "Does test anxiety bias scholastic aptitude test performance by gender and sociocultural group?" *Journal of Personality Assessment* 55, nos. 1–2 (Fall 1990): 145–60.

———. *Test anxiety: The state of the art.* New York: Plenum Press, 1998.

Conclusion

Burns, W. J., and P. Slovic. "Risk perception and behaviors: Anticipating and responding to crises." *Risk Analysis* 32, no. 4 (Apr. 2012): 579–82. doi: 10.1111/j.1539-6924.2012.01791.x.

Job, V., C. S. Dweck, and G. M. Walton. "Ego depletion—is it all in your head? Implicit theories about willpower affect self-regulation." *Psychological Science* 21, no. 11 (Nov. 2010): 1686–93. Epub Sep. 28, 2010.

Seery, M. "Resilience: A silver lining to experiencing adverse life events?" *Current Directions in Psychological Science* 20, no. 6 (Dec. 2011): 390–94.

Siegel, D. *The healing power of emotion: Affective neuroscience, development & clinical practice.* New York: W. W. Norton, 2009.

Slovic, P. "The construction of preference." *American Psychologist* 50 (1995): 364–71.

———. *The perception of risk.* London: Earthscan, 2000.

Slovic, P., M. Finucane, E. Peters, and D. MacGregor. "The affect heuristic." In T. Gilovich, D. Griffin, and D. Kahneman (eds.), *Intuitive judgement: Heuristics and biases.* Cambridge University Press, 2002.

Slovic, P., S. Lichtenstein, and B. Fischhof. "Decision making." In R. C. Atkinson, R. J. Lindzey, and R. D. Luce (eds.), *Handbook of experimental psychology.* New York: Wiley, 1988.

Index

Note: Page numbers in *italics* refer to illustrations.

Index

Index